T0114028

Cambridge Elements ≡

Elements in Publishing and Book Culture
edited by
Samantha Rayner
University College London
Rebecca Lyons
University of Bristol

PICTURE-BOOK PROFESSORS

Academia and Children's Literature

Melissa M. Terras
University of Edinburgh

The Element is also available, with additional material, as Open Access.

CAMBRIDGE
UNIVERSITY PRESS

University Printing House, Cambridge CB2 8BS, United Kingdom

One Liberty Plaza, 20th Floor, New York, NY 10006, USA

477 Williamstown Road, Port Melbourne, VIC 3207, Australia

314–321, 3rd Floor, Plot 3, Splendor Forum, Jasola District Centre,
New Delhi – 110025, India

79 Anson Road, #06–04/06, Singapore 079906

Cambridge University Press is part of the University of Cambridge.

It furthers the University's mission by disseminating knowledge in the pursuit of
education, learning, and research at the highest international levels of excellence.

www.cambridge.org
Information on this title: www.cambridge.org/9781108438452
DOI: 10.1017/9781108529501

When citing this work, please include a reference to the DOI 10.1017/9781108529501

First published 2018

A catalogue record for this publication is available from the British Library.

ISBN 978-1-108-43845-2 Paperback
ISSN 2514-8524 (online)
ISSN 2514-8516 (print)

The Element is also available, with additional material, as Open Access at
www.cambridge.org/Picture-Book-Professors

Cambridge Elements

Picture-Book Professors

Academia and Children's Literature

DOI: 10.1017/9781108529501

First published online: October 2018

Melissa M. Terras

ABSTRACT: How is academia portrayed in children's literature? This Element ambitiously surveys fictional professors in texts marketed towards children. Professors are overwhelmingly white and male, tending to be elderly scientists who fall into three stereotypes: the vehicle to explain scientific facts, the baffled genius, and the evil madman. By the late twentieth century, the stereotype of the male, mad, muddlehead, called Professor SomethingDumb, is formed in humorous yet pejorative fashion. This Element provides a publishing history of the role of academics in children's literature, questioning the book culture which promotes the enforcement of stereotypes regarding intellectual expertise in children's media.

The Element is also available, with additional material, as Open Access.

KEYWORDS: Children's Literature, Academia, English Literature, Gender Studies, Diversity, Representation

© Melissa M. Terras 2018

ISBNs: 9781108438452 (PB), 9781108529501 (OC)

ISSNs: 2514-8524 (online), 2514-8516 (print)

Contents

1 Introduction

How is academia portrayed in English language children's literature? From *The Water-Babies*[1] to *Tom Sawyer Abroad*,[2] *Professor Branestawm*,[3] *The Lion, the Witch and the Wardrobe*,[4] and on to *Northern Lights*[5] and the *Harry Potter* series,[6] professors are established as central characters in children's books: yet this role has been hitherto unexamined. In this ambitious Element, the representation of fictional academics – individuals teaching or researching within a university or higher education context, or with titles that denote a high rank within the academic sector – is analysed, concentrating on illustrated texts marketed towards children. Focussing on graphic depictions of fictional academics allows the gathering of a corpus which enables a longitudinal analysis: 328 academics were found in 289 different English language children's illustrated books published between 1850 and 2014, allowing trends to be identified using a mixed-method approach of both qualitative and quantitative analysis of overall bibliographic record, individual text and illustration. This establishes a publishing history of the role of academics in children's literature, while highlighting and questioning the book culture which promotes the construction and

---

[1] C. Kingsley, *The Water-Babies: A Fairy Tale for a Land-Baby*, 1885 edition illustrated by Linley Sambourne (London: Macmillan and Co., 1863, 1885).

[2] M. Twain, *Tom Sawyer Abroad* (London: Chatto and Windus, 1894).

[3] N. Hunter, *The Incredible Adventures of Professor Branestawm* (Harmondsworth: Penguin, 1933).

[4] C. S. Lewis, *The Lion, the Witch and the Wardrobe* (London: Geoffrey Bles, 1950).

[5] P. Pullman, *Northern Lights*. 'His Dark Materials' series, volume 1 (London: Scholastic Children's Books, 1995).

[6] J. K. Rowling, *Harry Potter and the Philosopher's Stone*. 'Harry Potter' series, volume 1 (London: Bloomsbury, 1997).

enforcement of stereotypes regarding intellectual expertise in media marketed towards children.

It is academics – teachers and scholars within a higher education setting – rather than other mentions of the university which come to represent the academy in children's literature: mentions of institutions or their associated structures or customs are rare. The appearance of fictional academics is closely tied to the history of higher education, with the earliest occurrences coinciding with the public funding and growth of the university sector in the latter part of the Victorian period. From then on, fictional academics appear regularly in children's books, and feature in popular and enduring texts. The incidence of professors in children's illustrated books increases over the latter half of the twentieth century, although this is closely linked to the fact that there are simply more children's books being produced within this timeframe. The academics are overwhelmingly white and male and tend to be elderly scientists. Fictional professors can be used as a device to explain and instruct in both fact and fiction. Professors and academic doctors coalesce into three distinct stereotypes: the kindly teacher who is little more than a vehicle to explain scientific facts; the baffled genius who is incapable of functioning in a normative societal manner; and the evil madman who is intent on destruction and mayhem. By the latter part of the twentieth century, the stereotype of the male, mad, muddlehead with absurd hair, called Professor SomethingDumb, is so strong that academics in children's literature are overwhelmingly presented as such without backstory or explanation. Experts, intellect and higher education are routinely presented as either slapstick or terrifying, in humorous yet pejorative fashion to the child reader, although there is also a trope of the trusted pedagogue or wise old man. These developed stereotypes also establish constraints around which authors and illustrators can easily build characterisation and plotlines and allow publishers to pigeonhole and market texts.

It is first useful to understand how different professions have been studied in children's literature, focussing on the closest sector that has received some attention: scientists. Next, the method is presented, looking at identifying, accessing and then classifying the texts in a methodological fashion. The *corpus*[7] is detailed, giving an overview of the 289 books, and looking at societal and commercial factors underpinning the growth of occurrences of professors in children's literature over this period of study. *Distant reading*[8] of bibliometric data – quantitative computational analysis of descriptions of books in the corpus – is combined with traditional close reading practices: a content analysis of the

[7] A term commonly used in humanities research to denote a curated collection of written texts, particularly the entire body of writing of a particular author, or on a given subject, which can be used for literary or linguistic study. For an overview of corpus construction methods, see J. Sinclair, 'Corpus and Text – Basic Principles', in M. Wynne (ed.), *Developing Linguistic Corpora: A Guide to Good Practice* (Oxford: Oxbow Books, 2005), pp. 1–16, http://ota.ox.ac.uk/documents/creating/dlc/.

[8] *Distant reading* is the effort to understand literature by aggregating and analysing large datasets, as opposed to close reading, which is a careful interpretation of a particular section of text. For the mutual relationship between corpora, computational analysis and close reading, see F. Moretti, *Distant Reading* (London:Verso Books, 2013), and also J. Rosen, 'Combining Close and Distant, or, the Utility of Genre Analysis: A Response to Matthew Wilkens's "Contemporary Fiction by the Numbers"' (3 December 2011), Post 45, http://post45.research.yale.edu/2011/12/combining-close-and-distant-or-the-utility-of-genre-analysis-a-response-to-matthew-wilkenss-contemporary-fiction-by-the-numbers/, T. Underwood, 'A Genealogy of Distant Reading', *Digital Humanities Quarterly*, Volume 11(2) (2017), www.digitalhumanities.org/dhq/vol/11/2/000317/000317.html, and K. Bode, 'The Equivalence of "Close" and "Distant" Reading; Or, Towards a New Object for Data-Rich Literary History', *Modern Language Quarterly* (December 2017); for the relationship of distant reading to the study of children's literature, see E. Giddens, 'Children's Literature and Distant Reading', in M. Nikolajeva and C. Beauvais (eds.), *The Edinburgh Companion to Children's Literature* (Edinburgh: Edinburgh University Press, 2017) pp. 305–13.

gathered collection guides attention to areas likely to repay individual focus. The striking heteronormative, patriarchal, white, scientific, maleness of academics in children's literature is revealed, underscoring previously undertaken research into the lack of diversity in children's literature, while also showing how stereotypes of academics fossilise and concentrate, becoming increasingly hard to break out from in modern texts. Turning to enduring and popular representations of academics in children's books, these stereotypes become blueprints for others to follow, or to deliberately fight against.

Representations of academics are tied to wider societal influences, including the depiction of celebrities such as Einstein, popular culture references to book, film and television such as *Frankenstein*, the resulting public perception of science and scientists, and, more broadly, the 'cult of ignorance'[9] in a society which has 'had enough of experts'.[10] The corpus demonstrates that, even to a preschool audience, illustrated books are describing advanced learning, intellectual excellence and academic achievement as something to be either feared or laughed at. The ramifications of this for their readership are unknown and unproven. However, the lack of diversity and the mocking nature, showing both the narrow perception of who is allowed intellectual agency in the fictional academy, and what little respect it should be given, potentially impacts the child reader, given previous studies into the effect of negative gender representation in children's books. It is possible to scope out probable effects of this, and point to how children's literature can both increase its diversity and step away from damaging stereotypes. In addition, the corpus of texts that have built up over the past century and a half are a lasting testament to the societal undercurrents of patriarchy, uniformity and anti-intellectualism, and how we teach our

---

[9] I. Asimov, 'A Cult of Ignorance', *Newsweek* (21 January 1980), p. 19.

[10] H. Mance, 'Britain has had enough of experts, says Gove', *Financial Times* (3 June 2016), www.ft.com/content/3be49734-29cb-11e6-83e4-abc22d5d108c.

children to understand these cultural infrastructures. Although this survey concentrates on professors in children's literature, it is likely that a similar study on different professions would show alarmingly interchangeable results (except vocations in which women have been traditionally 'allowed' to excel: teaching, nursing and librarianship[11]). The corpus has a complex, and sometimes uncomfortable, relationship with its real-life counterpart, simultaneously mirroring, mocking and reinforcing the lack of diversity in the actual academy.

This study pushes the affordances of digital methods, expanding established research methodologies and showing opportunities for others undertaking longitudinal, corpus-based work on changing representations in the study of children's literature. It is demonstrated that social media tools can be of benefit in the identification of texts to build up large-scale corpora, as well as making use of established methods of library catalogue searching and chaining. Access to digitised texts, particularly those in the public domain and those digitised on demand, improves the range of material that can be included in longitudinal corpora (although copyright restrictions mean a paucity of digitised twentieth-century texts can be obtainable legally). In addition, this research also highlights difficulties in navigating the current state of print-on-demand texts and ebooks, whilst demonstrating opportunities for studying children's literature at scale, over a long timeframe, using bibliographic data. It is shown that a mixed-method quantitative and qualitative approach can be used to allow both distant and close reading of texts, allowing trends and tropes to be identified, scrutinised and explained, in a 'genre study' that 'oscillates between levels of

---

[11] See C. Goldin, 'A Pollution Theory of Discrimination: Male and Female Differences in Occupations and Earnings', in *Human Capital in History: The American Record* (University of Chicago Press, 2014), pp. 313–348.

analysis, training its vision on a constellation of objects then telescoping in for a closer look' (Rosen, 'Combining Close and Distant'), this research, then, explores novel methods that may be useful for others in children's literature studies, and those undertaking longitudinal analyses of popular culture.

Relevant literature, including research into representation in children's literature and the portrayal of higher education in other media, is surveyed in Section 2. The research approach adopted here, including gathering and analysing the corpus, is presented in Section 3. Section 4 details the results of the analysis, looking at the historical growth of academics in illustrated children's literature and the main stereotypes that emerge regarding gender, race, class, appearance, subject matter and plot. The main behavioural stereotypes – those of the teacher, the baffled blunderer and the evil madman – are discussed in Section 5, while stereotypes are also presented as a framework for modern children's authors and illustrators to build upon. The influences on the construction of characters are detailed, including the representation of scientists in popular media, the building of the stereotype via popular and enduring works of children's literature, the influence on the representation of fictional academics by the constitution (and public perception) of the real-life university sector, and the wider socio-political media climate that fosters anti-intellectualism and populist rhetoric, revealing a complex network of associations referenced by authors and illustrators when depicting academics in children's literature. Finally, the findings are summarised in Section 6, which questions the dominance of the male, mad, muddlehead, asking what can be done to challenge the stereotype, while discussing limitations of this research, and areas for future study. Many of the early examples discussed in this analysis have also been made available in an open access anthology.[12]

---

[12] M. Terras, *The Professor in Children's Literature: An Anthology* (London: Fincham Press, 2018).

It is hoped that by carrying out this analysis, we can start to ask what we are teaching our children when it comes to experts and intellectual agency. The ridiculous parallel nature of our societal structures – the pale, male and stale universities[13] – and how we reinforce them to our children – the male, mad, muddlehead of children's literature – are revealed. We can see how children's literature responds to and, consciously or unconsciously, echoes societal trends in education, politics, history and popular culture. Looking at such a publishing history raises issues of the role of authors, illustrators and publishers in both utilising and standing up to established pejorative stereotypes within the children's book industry. Need fictional representations – which provide an extension of the world to our children – reinforce negative stereotypes so slavishly? Do these representations encourage us to ask difficult questions about the current constitution of the real-life academy? What can authors, illustrators and publishers do to address these issues? We can see where the shorthand of the male, mad, muddlehead professor emerges from, and then, hopefully, we can – in even a small way – challenge it.

2 Related Research: Representation, Vocation and Higher Education

Although no prior longitudinal analysis of academics and the university in children's literature has been found, there are various approaches, methods and observations that informed this research. Essentially, this is a study of representation within children's literature, and there is much prior work done in developing methods in which to identify, classify and analyse specific factors in children's

---

[13] See M. Flinders, F. Matthews and C. Eason, 'Are Public Bodies Still "Male, Pale and Stale"? Examining Diversity in UK Public Appointments 1997–2010', *Politics*, 31(3) (2011), pp. 129–139.

books: these are briefly surveyed. Such analyses are important given the effects that dominant narratives can have on child development: an overview is given of material that investigates this link, indicating why this type of study matters. Previously published research on professions in children's literature is summarised, followed by work undertaken which analyses scientists both in books written for a childhood audience and the wider media landscape, including work on how academia is presented in media targeted towards older audiences (including comic books, and popular culture). Although there is no published work on academics in children's literature, there is a wealth of methods that can be adopted and adapted from these prior studies.

2.1 The Study of Representation in Children's Literature

Before considering the portrayal of academics in children's books, it is useful to survey the long history of the study of representation in children's literature. Representation studies – focussing on the analysis of particular aspects featured in children's literature by: their illustration; the tone and word choice used in textual description; and how these two interact – are usually targeted towards broad measures such as gender,[14] ethnic diversity and cultural

---

[14] A. P. Nilsen, 'Women in Children's Literature', *College English*, 32(8) (1971), 918–926, http://doi.org/10.2307/375631; K. E. Heintz, 'An Examination of Sex and Occupational-Role Presentations of Female Characters in Children's Picture Books', *Women's Studies in Communication*, 10(2), (1987), 67–78; J. W. Stewig and R. Theilheimer, 'Men in Picture Books and Environments', *Early Childhood Education Journal*, 19(4), (1992), 38–43; S. C. Saad, 'The Gender of Chronically Ill Characters in Children's Realistic Fiction, 1970–1994', *Sexuality and Disability*, 17(1), (1999), 79–92; C. Brugeilles, I. Cromer, S. Cromer and Z. Andreyev, 'Male and Female Characters in Illustrated Children's Books or How Children's Literature Contributes to the Construction of Gender', *Population (English Edition)*, (2002), 237–267; R. Clark, J. Guilmain, P. K. Saucier and J. Tavarez, 'Two Steps Forward, One Step

identity,[15] parental roles,[16] sexuality[17] and disability.[18] Qualitative and

Back: The Presence of Female Characters and Gender Stereotyping in Award-Winning Picture Books between the 1930s and the 1960s', *Sex Roles*, 49(9–10), (2003), 439–449; C. Hendricks, J. Hendricks, T. Messenheimer, M. S. Houston and J. Williford, 'Exploring Occupational Stereotypes in Children's Picture Books', *International Journal of the Book*, 7(2), (2010); H. Rao and H. Smith, 'The Representation of Women Doctors in Children's Picture Books', *Journal of the Royal Society of Medicine*, 107(12), (2014), 480–482.

[15] L. Edmonds, 'The Treatment of Race in Picture Books for Young Children', *Book Research Quarterly*, 2(3), (1986), 30–41; M. Cai, 'Images of Chinese and Chinese Americans Mirrored in Picture Books', *Children's Literature in Education*, 25(3), (1994), 169–191; M. D. Koss, 'Diversity in Contemporary Picturebooks: A Content Analysis', *Journal of Children's Literature*, 41(1), (2015), 32; S. J. Wee, S. Park and J. S. Choi, 'Korean Culture as Portrayed in Young Children's Picture Books: The Pursuit of Cultural Authenticity', *Children's Literature in Education*, 46(1), (2015), 70–87; Centre for Literacy in Primary Education (CLPE), 'Survey of Ethnic Representation within UK Children's Literature 2017' (2018) clpe.org.uk/library-and-resources/research/reflecting-realities-survey-ethnic-representation-within-uk-children.

[16] D. A. Anderson and M. Hamilton, 'Gender Role Stereotyping of Parents in Children's Picture Books: The Invisible Father', *Sex Roles*, 52(3–4), (2005), 145–151; A. L. DeWitt, C. M. Cready and R. R. Seward, 'Parental Role Portrayals in Twentieth Century Children's Picture Books: More Egalitarian or Ongoing Stereotyping?', *Sex Roles*, 69(1–2), (2013), 89–106; V. Joosen, '"Look More Closely,' Said Mum": Mothers in Anthony Browne's Picture Books', *Children's Literature in Education* 46(2) (2015), 145–159.

[17] J. Schall and G. Kauffmann, 'Exploring Literature with Gay and Lesbian Characters in the Elementary School', *Journal of Children's Literature*, 29(1), (2003), 36–45; J. Sapp, 'A Review of Gay and Lesbian Themed Early Childhood Children's Literature', *Australasian Journal of Early Childhood*, 35(1), (2010), 32; C. L. Ryan and J. M. Hermann-Wilmarth, 'Already on the Shelf: Queer Readings of Award-Winning Children's Literature', *Journal of Literacy Research*, 45(2), (2013), 142–172.

[18] S. A. Wagoner, 'The Portrayal of the Cognitively Disabled in Children's Literature', *The Reading Teacher*, 37(6), (1984), 502–508; Saad, 'The Gender of Chronically Ill Characters in Children's Realistic Fiction'; N. Matthew and S. Clow, 'Putting

quantitative analyses reveal time and time again that children's literature is severely lacking in all areas of diversity.[19] Representational analysis is also used to study subjects in children's literature as diverse as behavioural issues,[20] school environments,[21] bereavement,[22] Art Museums[23] and the appearance of objects such as the moon.[24]

These previous studies, which often analyse written and visual text in both qualitative and quantitative approaches, informed the methodology. The number of books analysed varies, depending also on the methods used: from close reading – with two books,[25] four,[26] thirteen,[27]

Disabled Children in the Picture: Promoting Inclusive Children's Books and Media', *International Journal of Early Childhood*, 39(2), (2007), 65–78.

[19] P. Nel and L. Paul, eds., *Keywords for Children's Literature* (New York, NY: NYU Press, 2011).

[20] P. A. Oppliger and A. Davis, 'Portrayals of Bullying: A Content Analysis of Picture Books for Preschoolers', *Early Childhood Education Journal* (2015), 1–12.

[21] E. C. Phillips and B. W. Sturm, 'Do Picture Books About Starting Kindergarten Portray the Kindergarten Experience in Developmentally Appropriate Ways?', *Early Childhood Education Journal*, 41(6), (2013), 465–475.

[22] K. D. Malafantis, 'Death Shall Have No Dominion: Representations of Grandfathers' Death in Contemporary Picturebooks', *Advances in Literary Study*, 1(4), (2013), 34.

[23] E. Yohlin, 'Pictures in Pictures: Art History and Art Museums in Children's Picture Books', *Children's Literature in Education*, 43(3), (2012), 260–272.

[24] K. C. Trundle, T. H. Troland and T. G. Pritchard, 'Representations of the Moon in Children's Literature: An Analysis of Written and Visual Text', *Journal of Elementary Science Education*, 20(1), (2008), 17–28.

[25] Malafantis, 'Death Shall Have No Dominion'.

[26] Yohlin, 'Pictures in Pictures'; Joosen, '"Look More Closely," Said Mum'.

[27] Stewig and Theilheimer, 'Men in Picture Books and Environments'; Phillips and Sturm, 'Do Picture Books about Starting Kindergarten Portray the Kindergarten Experience in Developmentally Appropriate Ways?'.

fourteen[28]– to the use of qualitative methods – with twenty-two books,[29] twenty-five books,[30] thirty-three,[31] thirty-seven,[32] seventy-three,[33] seventy-four,[34] seventy-eight,[35] eighty,[36] eighty-four,[37] ninety-one,[38] 100,[39] 111,[40] 200,[41] 300,[42]

[28] Heintz, 'An Examination of Sex and Occupational-Role Presentations of Female Characters in Children's Picture Books'.

[29] A. M. Allen, D. N. Allen and G. Sigler, 'Changes in Sex-Role Stereotyping in Caldecott Medal Award Picture Books 1938–1988', *Journal of Research in Childhood Education*, 7(2), (1993), 67–73.

[30] Hendricks, Hendricks, Messenheimer, Houston and Williford, 'Exploring Occupational Stereotypes in Children's Picture Books'.

[31] Wee, Park and Choi, 'Korean Culture as Portrayed in Young Children's Picture Books'.

[32] P. Mudhovozi, 'Sex-Role Stereotyping in the Infant Learners' Picture Book', *Journal of Social Sciences*, 44(1), (2015), 87–90.

[33] Cai, 'Images of Chinese and Chinese Americans Mirrored in Picture Books'.

[34] M. J. Kashey, 'Occupation and Activity Gender Trends in the Berenstain Bear Series', ERIC Document ED374470 (1993), from https://eric.ed.gov/?id=ED374470.

[35] Saad, 'The Gender of Chronically Ill Characters in Children's Realistic Fiction'.

[36] Nilsen, 'Women in Children's Literature'; Trundle, Troland and Pritchard, 'Representations of the Moon in Children's Literature'.

[37] Clark, Guilmain, Saucier and Tavarez, 'Two Steps Forward, One Step Back'.

[38] S. F. Amass, 'Representations of the Veterinary Profession in Nonfiction Children's Books', *Journal of the American Veterinary Medical Association*, 238(9), (2011), 1126–1131.

[39] Oppliger and Davis, 'Portrayals of Bullying'.

[40] C. H. Rawson and M. A. McCool, 'Just Like All the Other Humans? Analyzing Images of Scientists in Children's Trade Books', *School Science and Mathematics* 114 (1), (2014), 10–18.

[41] Anderson and Hamilton, 'Gender Role Stereotyping of Parents in Children's Picture Books'; M. C. Hamilton, D. Anderson, M. Broaddus and K. Young, 'Gender Stereotyping and Under-Representation of Female Characters in 200 Popular Children's Picture Books: A Twenty-First Century Update', *Sex Roles*, 55(11–12), (2006), 757–765.

[42] DeWitt, Cready and Seward, 'Parental Role Portrayals in Twentieth Century Children's Picture Books'.

455,[43] 537[44] and 952.[45] Given the relatively large size of our corpus, a mixed method approach was both helpful and required, looking to the studies that carried out an analysis of over seventy books, using a content analysis methodology detailed in Section 3.

2.2 Why Study Representation in Children's Literature?

Why does it matter to study such representation and to identify stereotypes? Entertainment media affects the behaviour, ethical approach, perspective, outlook and conduct of consumers.[46] Much research into diversity in children's literature assumes stereotypes are bad without explaining their mechanisms or the evidence that exists for their negative affect on child development. To counter this, Peterson and Lach[47] surveyed previously publicised research into the effects of gender stereotyping in children's books on child development, showing 'that the reading materials to which we expose children shape their attitudes, their understanding and their behaviour',[48] indicating that stereotypes

---

[43] Koss, 'Diversity in Contemporary Picturebooks'.

[44] Brugeilles, Cromer, Cromer and Andreyev, 'Male and Female Characters in Illustrated Children's Books'.

[45] Edmonds, 'The Treatment of Race in Picture Books for Young Children'.

[46] See D. Kellner, 'Towards a Critical Media/Cultural Studies', in R. Hammer and D. Kellner (eds.), *Media/Cultural Studies: Critical Approaches* (New York, NY: Peter Lang Publishing, 2009), pp. 5–24 for an overview.

[47] S. B. Peterson and M. A. Lach, 'Gender Stereotypes in Children's Books: Their Prevalence and Influence on Cognitive and Affective Development', *Gender and Education*, 2(2), (1990), pp. 185–197.

[48] Ibid., p. 188.

may impair the development of positive self-concepts, and induce negative attitudes towards the child's own developmental potential and toward that of other children. They may significantly alter the child's cognitive development, presenting them with an inaccurate and potentially destructive world-view ... Educators would seem to bear a special responsibility in facilitating further change.[49]

Likewise, Steyer[50] updates this survey of research into the effects of gender stereotyping on children, including television, film, books, video games and the Internet, showing that negative portrayals had 'a negative effect on female self-efficacy'.[51] Research into the effects of other stereotypes is in its infancy but is expected to closely follow these findings associated with gender stereotypes, and, indeed, the very threat of being judged negatively due to stereotypes affects performance.[52] Negative stereotypes can be subverted; for example, 'exposure to non-sexist gender portrayals may be associated with a decrease in stereotypical beliefs about gender roles'.[53] The success of 'media literacy education to reduce the media's role in perpetuating stereotypes – training people in the skills to "interpret, analyse, and critique" negative

[49] Ibid.

[50] I. Steyer, 'Gender Representations in Children's Media and their Influence', *Campus-Wide Information Systems*, 31(2/3), (2014), 171–180, https://dx.doi.org/10.1108/CWIS-11-2013-0065.

[51] Ibid., p. 175.

[52] S. J. Spencer, C. Logel and P. G. Davies, 'Stereotype Threat', *Annual Review of Psychology*, 67, (2016), 415–437.

[53] Steyer, 'Gender Representations in Children's Media and their Influence', p. 175.

stereotypes ' – is not yet well evidenced,[54] but it offers a potential source of intervention into the perpetration of bias.[55] Understanding the source, mechanism and prevalence of representational stereotypes helps unpack their power and provides a means by which to critique and suggest alternatives. The study presented here aims to provide an analysis of how academia is portrayed in children's literature, in the hope we can both understand, improve and learn from it.

2.3 Analysis of Vocations in Children's Literature

Analysing diversity in children's literature, or the lack thereof, is a major contemporary topic for the research community.[56] Previous work analysing the representation of different professions in children's books focuses on

[54] E. Scharrer and S. Ramasubramanian, 'Intervening in the Media's Influence on Stereotypes of Race and Ethnicity: The Role of Media Literacy Education', *Journal of Social Issues*, 71(1), (2015), 171–185, p. 182.

[55] Ibid.

[56] For recent work see R. Bittner and M. Superle, 'The Still Almost All-White World of Children's Literature: Theory, Practice, and Identity-Based Children's Book Awards', in K. B. Kidd and J. T. Thomas (eds.), P*rizing Children's Literature: The Cultural Politics of Children's Book Awards* (New York, NY: Taylor & Francis, 2017), pp. 87–103; M. E. Friddle, 'Who is a "Girl"? The Tomboy, the Lesbian, and the Transgender Child', in T. Clasen and H. Hassel (eds.), *Gender(ed) Identities, Critical Rereadings of Gender in Children's and Young Adult Literature* (New York, NY: Routledge, 2017), pp. 117–134; R. Long, 'Freedom in Fantasy? Gender Restrictions in Children's Literature', in T. Clasen and H. Hassel (eds.), *Gender(ed) Identities, Critical Rereadings of Gender in Children's and Young Adult Literature* (New York, NY: Routledge, 2017), pp. 281–294; A. Ventura, 'Prizing the Unrecognized: Systems of Value, Visibility, and the First World in International and Translated Children's Texts', in K. B. Kidd and J. T. Thomas (eds.), *Prizing Children's Literature: The Cultural Politics of Children's Book Awards* (New York, NY: Routledge, 2017), pp. 32–44.

occupational gender stereotypes[57] and how they have changed over time: Allen et al.[58] found a weak trend towards more egalitarian representation, although males are more likely to be characterized as 'active, outdoors, and non-traditional ... in diverse occupations more often than females'.[59] Tangentially, a strand of research also follows, considering how occupational stereotypes are perceived by, and affect, children.[60] The representation of individual, specific vocations in children's picture books has received relatively limited attention, the focus instead having been primarily on distinct professions identifiable to

[57] Heintz, 'An Examination of Sex and Occupational-Role Presentations of Female Characters in Children's Picture Books'; Kashey, 'Occupation and Activity Gender Trends in the Berenstain Bear Series'; Hamilton, Anderson, Broaddus and Young, 'Gender Stereotyping and Under-Representation of Female Characters in 200 Popular Children's Picture Books'; Hendricks, Hendricks, Messenheimer, Houston and Williford, 'Exploring Occupational Stereotypes in Children's Picture Books'; Mudhovozi, 'Sex-Role Stereotyping in the Infant Learners' Picture Book'.

[58] Allen, Allen and Sigler, 'Changes in Sex-Role Stereotyping in Caldecott Medal Award Picture Books'.

[59] Ibid., p. 67.

[60] M. S. Ashby and B. C. Wittmaier, 'Attitude Changes in Children After Exposure to Stories about Women in Traditional or Nontraditional Occupations', *Journal of Educational Psychology*, 70(6), (1978), 945; D. A. Rosenthal and D. C. Chapman, 'The Lady Spaceman: Children's Perceptions of Sex-Stereotyped Occupations', *Sex Roles*, 8(9), (1982), 959–965; M. L. Trepanier-Street and J. A. Romatowski, 'The Influence of Children's Literature on Gender Role Perceptions: A Reexamination', *Early Childhood Education Journal*, 26(3), (1999), 155–159; L. S. Liben, R. S. Bigler and H. R. Krogh, 'Language at Work: Children's Gendered Interpretations of Occupational Titles', *Child Development*, 73(3), (2002), 810–828_1595403505.

children, such as doctors,[61] veterinarians,[62] librarians,[63] farmers,[64] soldiers[65] and teachers.[66] These studies examined various areas such as gender, ethnic diversity (the lack of diversity in both gender and race is a common cause for concern) and characteristics of the individuals portrayed, to look at both the

[61] N. Van Ginneken, 'Missionary Doctors in Children's Literature: Africa, India and China: c. 1880 to c. 1950', Doctoral dissertation (Wellcome Institute for the History of Medicine, 1999); M. Lalanda and J. A. Alonso, 'Daisy the Doctor, Dr Dose, Dr Grizzly, Dr Amelia Bedelia, and Colleagues', *British Medical Journal*, 333(7582), (2006), 1330–1332; Rao and Smith, 'The Representation of Women Doctors in Children's Picture Books'.

[62] Amass, 'Representations of the Veterinary Profession in Nonfiction Children's Books'.

[63] D. N. Bowen, 'The Image of Libraries and Librarians in Children's Literature', *Kentucky Libraries*, 67(4), (2003), 8–10; E. Yontz, 'Librarians in Children's Literature, 1909–2000', *The Reference Librarian*, 37(78), (2003), 85–96; S. Maynard and F. McKenna, 'Mother Goose, Spud Murphy and the Librarian Knights: Representations of Librarians and their Libraries in Modern Children's Fiction', *Journal of Librarianship and Information Science*, 37(3), (2005), 119–129.

[64] M. Kruse, 'Aprons, Overalls, and So Much More: Images of Farm Workers in Children's Picture Books', *Journal of Children's Literature*, 27(2), (2001), 22–28; S. A. Beck, 'Children of Migrant Farmworkers in Picture Storybooks: Reality, Romanticism, and Representation', *Children's Literature Association Quarterly*, 34(2), (2009), 99–137.

[65] C. M. Desai, 'Picture Book Soldiers: Men and Messages', *Reading Horizons*, 42(2), (2001), 77–98; E. A. Galway, 'Competing Representations of Boy Soldiers in WWI Children's Literature', *Peace Review*, 24(3), (2012), 298–304.

[66] D. Barone, 'Images of Teachers in Children's Literature', *New Advocate*, 8(4), (1995), 257–270; S. J. Sandefur and L. Moore, 'The "Nuts and Dolts" of Teacher Images in Children's Picture Storybooks: A Content Analysis', *Education*, 125(1), (2004), 41; J. E. P. Brady, 'The Portrayal of Caring Teachers in Children's Literature'. Doctoral dissertation (Washington State University, 2009); S. Dockett, B. Perry and D. Whitton, 'What Will My Teacher Be Like?: Picture Storybooks about Starting School', *Australasian Journal of Early Childhood*, 35(3), (September 2010), 33–41; J. L. C. Yau, 'The Representation of Teachers in Taiwanese Children's Literature, 1960–2012', *Children's Literature in Education*, 46(3), (2015), 308–324.

explicit and implicit messages about these professions that the illustrations and text were conveying.

Of greatest interest is previous work done on the representation of scientists in children's literature (in both fiction and nonfiction): it should be borne in mind that scientists are not all academics, and academics are not all scientists, but there is some understandable overlap between the two, and previous studies proved useful to this approach. Rawson and McCool examined images of 1657 scientists in 111 nonfiction juvenile trade books, demonstrating that 'Scientists in these books are shown in a wide variety of settings and are largely missing stereotypical features'; however, 'the standard image of the scientist as a White male is still perpetuated in these titles, and this is a cause for concern'. [67] Van Gorp et al. looked at the representation of scientists in a range of books and comics aimed at Dutch children and teenagers, identifying seven main stereotypes: 'the genius, the nerd, the puzzler, the adventurer, the mad scientist, the wizard, and the misunderstood genius',[68] stressing that scientists in children's fiction were generally more stereotypically eccentric, undertaking more risky, useless experiments than those in factual texts. Similar findings emerged from Van Gorp and Rommes' study of scientists in Belgian comic books.[69] There has been a great deal of work done on the representation of scientists in media marketed towards adults, including literature[70] and film and

[67] Rawson and McCool, 'Just Like All the Other Humans?', pp. 16–17.

[68] B. Van Gorp, E. Rommes and P. Emons, 'From the Wizard to the Doubter: Prototypes of Scientists and Engineers in Fiction and Non-Fiction Media Aimed at Dutch Children and Teenagers', *Public Understanding of Science*, 23(6), (2014), 646–659, p. 651.

[69] B. Van Gorp and E. Rommes, 'Scientists in Belgian Comics: Typology, Chronology and Origins', *Journal of Graphic Novels and Comics*, 5(2), (2014), 154–169.

[70] M. Millhauser, 'Dr. Newton and Mr. Hyde: Scientists in Fiction from Swift to Stevenson', *Nineteenth-Century Fiction*, 28(3), (1973), 287–304; D. Bevan, (ed.), *University Fiction*, Vol. 5 (Rodopi, 1990); R. D. Haynes, *From Faust to Strangelove:*

television,[71] which will contribute to the discussion of the research findings: scientists in fiction are generally old, white males[72] with a master narrative of the scientist as a bad and dangerous person linked to societal fears regarding the impact of technological change, which is particularly pronounced after the Second World War.[73]

Representations of the Scientist in Western Literature (Baltimore and London: The Johns Hopkins University Press, 1994); R. Haynes, 'From Alchemy to Artificial Intelligence: Stereotypes of the Scientist in Western Literature', *Public Understanding of Science*, 12(3), (2003), 243–253; K. Roach, 'Between Magic and Reason: Science in 19th Century Popular Fiction', Doctoral dissertation (University of Nottingham, 2011); D. Mosler and J. Murrell, 'Historians in Fiction and Film', in T. Gibbons and E. Sutherland (eds.), *Integrity and Historical Research* (Taylor and Francis, 2011), 187–204; H. Merrick, 'Challenging Implicit Gender Bias in Science: Positive Representations of Female Scientists in Fiction', *Journal of Community Positive Practices*, 12(4), (2012), 744.

[71] P. Weingart, 'Chemists and their Craft in Fiction Film', in J. Schummer, B. Bensaude-Vincent and B. Van Tiggelen (eds.), *The Public Image of Chemistry* (World Scientific, 2007), pp. 81–96; A. R. Franzini, 'Is School Cool? Representations of Academics and Intelligence on Teen Television', in L. Holderman (ed.), *Common Sense: Intelligence as Presented on Popular Television* (Lanham, MD: Lexington Books, 2008), pp. 187–198; B. Blankenship, 'The Female Professor on Film', *The Montana Professor*, 21(1), (Fall 2010), http://mtprof.msun.edu/Fall2010/film.html; J. J. Williams, 'The Thrill is Gone: Recent Films Portray the Malaise of Academic Life', *Chronicle of Higher Education* (14 February 2010), http://chronicle.com/article/Just-Like-in-the-Movies/64109/; L. A. Orthia and R. Morgain, 'The Gendered Culture of Scientific Competence: A Study of Scientist Characters in Doctor Who 1963–2013', *Sex Roles*, 75(3–4), (August 2016), 1–16.

[72] M. C. LaFollette, *Making Science Our Own: Public Images of Science, 1910–1955* (Chicago, IL: University of Chicago Press, 1990).

[73] Haynes, 'From Alchemy to Artificial Intelligence'.

2.4 Analysis of Higher Education in Popular Culture

Previous analysis of depictions of higher education in popular culture suggests

> the dominance of straight white men, the lack of diversity, privileging certain types of institutions, and non-academic depictions contribute to anti-intellectual representations of higher education.[74]

---

[74] P. Reynolds, 'From Superman to Squirrel Girl: Higher Education in Comic Books, 1938–2015', in B. Tobolowsky and P. Reynolds (eds.), *Anti-Intellectual Representations of American Colleges and Universities: Fictional Higher Education*, Higher Education and Society Series (New York, NY: Springer, 2017), pp. 33–54, p. 51; see also S. Marchalonis, *College Girls: A Century in Fiction* (Piscataway Township, NJ: Rutgers University Press, 1995), B. F. Tobolowsky, 'Beyond Demographics: Understanding the College Experience through Television', *New Directions for Student Services*, 114, (2006), 17–26, L. Wasylkiw and M. Currie, 'The "Animal House" Effect: How University-Themed Comedy Films Affect Students' Attitudes', *Social Psychology of Education: An International Journal*, 15(1), (2012), 25–40, P. J. Reynolds, 'Representing "U": Popular Culture, Media, and Higher Education', *ASHE Higher Education Report*, 40(4), (2014), 1–145, T. Yakaboski and S. Donahoo, 'Hollywood's Representations of College Women and the Implications for Housing and Residence Life Professionals', *Journal of College & University Student Housing*, 41(2), (2015), J. De Groot, *Consuming History: Historians and Heritage in Contemporary Popular Culture* (London: Routledge, 2016), A. Ross, *No Respect: Intellectuals and Popular Culture* (Routledge, 2016), B. F. Tobolowsky and P. J. Reynolds (eds.), *Anti-Intellectual Representations of American Colleges and Universities: Fictional Higher Education* (New York, NY: Palgrave Macmillan, 2017) and P. Reynolds, '"Do You Want Me to Become a Social Piranha?": Smarts and Sexism in College Women's Representation in the US TV show, "Greek"' (forthcoming, 2017b) for further analyses of the depiction of universities and academics in fiction, film, news media and television.

Even the campus novel itself, analysed in Showalter, while usually 'sensational and apocalyptic',[75] adheres to these well-established hierarchies, dealing with anything that deviates from them in regard to sexuality or race in ways which are 'quirky, pedantic, vengeful, legalistic, and inhumane. The ivory towers have become fragile fortresses with glassy walls'.[76] There are well-established tropes of who gets to have intellectual agency within the fictional academy in books, television, and film, with gendered portrayals that 'unjustly and inaccurately privilege men within the context of a higher education environment'.[77]

The analysis of higher education in specific comic strips has been carried out, such as in *Tank McNamara*[78] and *Piled Higher and Deeper*.[79] A qualitative analysis of the representation of academia in American comic books published between 1938 and 2015 found examples of higher education, including settings and characters, in over 700 comic books, and purposively sampled them to analyse how Higher Education is depicted in general[80] and how professors are depicted specifically.[81] Expertise is the defining characteristic of comic book academics:

[75] E. Showalter, *Faculty Towers: The Academic Novel and its Discontents* (Oxford University Press, 2005), p. 148.

[76] Ibid., p. 146. [77] Reynolds, 'Do You Want Me to Become a Social Piranha?', p. 5.

[78] C. K. Harrison, S. M. Lawrence, M. Plecha, J. D. Scott Bukstein and N. K. Janson, 'Stereotypes and Stigmas of College Athletes in Tank McNamara's Cartoon Strip: Fact or Fiction?', *Journal of Issues in Intercollegiate Athletics*, Special Issue, 2009, 1–1, www.csri-jiia.org/old/documents/publications/specia l_issues/2009/sp_01_Cartoon_Article.pdf.

[79] F. Kelly, 'Supervision Satirized: Fictional Narratives of Student–Supervisor Relationships', *Arts and Humanities in Higher Education*, 8(3), (2009), 368–384.

[80] Reynolds, 'From Superman to Squirrel Girl'.

[81] P. Reynolds and S. D. DeMoss, 'Super Higher Education: The Role of Academics in Comic Books, 1938–2015', Society for Research into Higher Education, Annual

> Professors are established as the characters that innovate, dis-
> cover, examine and create both cutting edge technology and bold
> scientific experiments that are often needed to save the day.[82]

The dominance of STEM subjects is also identified, and the absence, or
grotesque portrayal of women, leading to

> possible percussions for the validity of an inclusive profession
> and non-differentiated expectations of students, or others, based
> on gender, race, and discipline.[83]

Interestingly, 'only rarely do professors deliberately work for nefarious
purposes',[84] puncturing any expectations of evil scientists. Reynolds[85] traces
the history of academia in comic books, finding both static and dynamic elements
of depiction of fictional higher education. College itself is 'a spaciously green, safe
space that doesn't really change ... connect[ing] with and bolster[ing] public
imaginings of US institutions of higher education' but 'depicting fictional institutions of indistinguishable type'.[86] The act of going to college provides a structural
narrative convention around which much action pivots. Students are a dominant
focus, but there are also many professors 'who are overwhelmingly male' that
'feature in narratives as main or supporting characters' acting 'as villains or rivals
in some comic book narratives'.[87] Women tend to have peripheral roles. Heroes
are all white 'but perhaps unsurprisingly, villains might not be',[88] and there is

Conference 7–9 December 2016, Newport, Wales, www.srhe.ac.uk/confer
ence2016/abstracts/0277.pdf.

[82] Ibid., p. 4. [83] Ibid., p. 7. [84] Ibid., p. 5.
[85] Reynolds, 'From Superman to Squirrel Girl'. [86] Ibid., p. 40. [87] Ibid., p. 45.
[88] Ibid., p. 49.

limited inclusion of diverse characteristics. Reynolds suggests that the 'blanket anti-intellectual discourse in media related to higher education' is replaced with 'more sophisticated understandings of these themes',[89] sometimes challenging, but sometimes reinforcing, anti-intellectual messages. These studies provide a useful counterpoint to the work presented here; however, many of the comics surveyed are produced for a much older age range than is focused upon in this analysis.

2.5 Analysis of Individual Children's Texts

There are a few analyses of individual academic scientists in children's fiction. For example, Smith's examination of the 'kindly' Professor Ptthmllnsprts ('Put them all in Spirits') from *The Water-Babies*[90] in his overview of the importance of science to the Victorian novel highlights how

> Even the well-meaning naturalist could become consumed by
> his interests to the detriment of his connections with, and
> responsibilities towards, family, friends and community.[91]

Ptthmllnsprts is considered 'a symbol of secular science . . . particularly illustrated by his obsession with collecting' in Talairach-Vielmas.[92] Giddens uses Ptthmllnsprts as a frame to discuss the illustration of science to a nineteenth-century childhood audience, showing how the adult body dominates depictions

---

[89] Ibid., p. 51. [90] Kingsley, *The Water-Babies*

[91] J. Smith, 'The Victorian Novel and Science', in L. Rodensky (ed.), *The Oxford Handbook of the Victorian Novel* (Oxford University Press, 2013), pp. 441–458, p. 446.

[92] L. Talairach-Vielmas, *Fairy Tales, Natural History and Victorian Culture* (Palgrave Macmillan, 2014), p. 42.

of science.[93] Bell's consideration of *Professor Branestawm*[94] looks at the 'ways in which images of children or the childlike are used in the construction of the scientist'.[95] Jafari[96] explores the Jungian archetype of the wise old man in *The Chronicles of Narnia*,[97] examining Professor Digory Kirke's role in temporally and intellectually framing the series from *The Lion, The Witch and The Wardrobe* onwards.[98] Much academic interest surrounds the *Harry Potter* series;[99] for example, see Heilman,[100] Whited[101] and Fenske,[102] with publications mentioning the professorial teachers at Hogwarts such as Birch, who demonstrates that Albus Dumbledore is a paragon: 'kind and gentle,

[93] E. Giddens, 'Ptthmllnsprts: Visualising Science in Nineteenth-Century Children's Fantasy', International Conference on the Fantastic in the Arts 2015, The Scientific Imagination, Orlando, Florida (18–22 March, 2015).

[94] Hunter, *The Incredible Adventures of Professor Branestawm*.

[95] A. Bell, 'The Incredible Adventures of Professor Branestawm: The Maturing Image of Science in 20th Century Juvenile Literature', in L. Locke and S. Locke (eds.), *Knowledges in Publics* (Cambridge Scholars Publishing, 2013), pp. 99–214, p. 199.

[96] B. M. Jafari, 'Exploring the Archetypes of Initiation and Wise Old Man in C. S. Lewis's The Chronicles of Narnia', Masters' thesis (Universiti Putra Malaysia, 2010).

[97] C. Jung, *Collected Works of C. G. Jung*, Vol. 9, Part 1, Second edition (Princeton University Press, 1968), pp. 217–230.

[98] Lewis, *The Lion, the Witch and the Wardrobe*.

[99] Rowling, *Harry Potter and the Philosopher's Stone* onwards.

[100] E. E. Heilman (ed.), *Harry Potter's World: Multidisciplinary Critical Perspectives* (New York, NY: RoutledgeFalmer, 2003).

[101] L. A. Whited, *The Ivory Tower and Harry Potter: Perspectives on a Literary Phenomenon* (University of Missouri Press, 2004).

[102] C. Fenske, *Muggles, Monsters and Magicians: A Literary Analysis of the Harry Potter Series*, Vol. 2 (Peter Lang, 2008).

energetic and wise, trusting and trusted, experienced and patient'[103] and that Minerva McGonagall's 'appearance, her personality, and her pedagogy conjure images of a stereotypical school-marm'.[104] However, Birch stresses the 'absence of intellectual work by teachers as well as the singular and completely school based identities',[105] and there is little consideration of the academic achievements or standing of the professors found in the Harry Potter critical literature (or, indeed, in the texts). Overall, considerations of lone academics are rare. There has been no prior overarching work found on trends and tropes in the representation of academics, more broadly framed, in children's literature.

2.6 Conclusion

The literature review has shown that there has been no prior overarching research on the representation of higher education in children's books, despite both the importance of these institutions to today's society, and the fact that academics (such as professors and non-medical or research doctors) feature in many popular and enduring works. Nowadays, university is an expected educational 'next step' for a large proportion of school-leavers in the Western world, and the lack of prior work on how academia is portrayed to a childhood audience through literature is therefore surprising. There are useful research methods that can be appropriated from the analysis of representation in children's literature and other media, and relevant prior work on how specific professions, including scientists, are portrayed and perceived in children's literature.

[103] M. L. Birch, 'Schooling Harry Potter: Teachers and Learning, Power and Knowledge', in E. E. Heilman (ed.), *Critical Perspectives on Harry Potter*, Second edition (Routledge, 2009), pp. 103–120, p. 113.

[104] Ibid., p. 108. [105] Ibid., p. 119.

Understanding the representation of the university sector in books marketed towards a young audience is important, given the effect stereotypes and portrayals have on children's actuation and development, and this analysis will reveal what messages are being portrayed to young children about intellectual achievement and higher education.

3 Research Methodology

What methods could be used to study how academics are depicted in children's literature? A search of English language children's books indicated that the people, rather than the places, are the focus of both fiction and non-fiction texts, and a methodology was developed to analyse illustrated fictional academics. This gathered core information on features of academics, using both textual references and analysis of illustrations. It is acknowledged that there are many more professors, doctors and researchers which appear in the text of books marketed towards children that *do not* have illustrations: the requirement for illustration also somewhat limits the corpus to a manageable size to facilitate a longitudinal study, while firmly focussing on texts produced for a young childhood audience. Illustrations also impart further information about the representation of academics than analysing textual descriptions alone, providing a rich corpus from which to draw upon.

There are two aspects to the method necessary for a study of this nature: first, the collection of the unique corpus, and second, the framework used to analyse it. Given the scope of this research, and the variety of texts identified for inclusion, clear decisions had to be made to guide both.

3.1 Building the Corpus

The corpus was constructed over a four-year period between April 2012 and April 2016, gathering all relevant texts possible that were published before the close of 2014. The gap between the end of the census and analysis allows for the fact that books often take a while to appear in library catalogues or other online environments. The use of digital resources was central to this task, facilitating the commonly used information seeking behaviour of starting, chaining, browsing, differentiating, monitoring and extracting[106] to identify relevant examples. Seed keywords included many terms related to academia (and their plurals): academic; academy; campus; college; degree; doctor; faculty; fraternity; fresher; freshman; graduate; graduation; lecturer; polytechnic; professor;[107] research; researcher; semester; sophomore; student; term; tutor; undergraduate; university; and varsity.[108] The irony is not lost here that searching for illustrated academics in children's books required textual searches: there is no current way to allow searching for aspects of academia that may be pictured, such as mortar boards or academic gowns and hoods, in illustrated texts, many of which are still in copyright and few of which are available in digital form. Such representations, without textual explanation, may also only be of old-fashioned schoolteachers (for example, this is surely the

---

[106] D. Ellis, 'A Behavioural Model for Information Retrieval System Design', *Journal of Information Science*, 15(4–5), (1989), 237–247.

[107] There are differences in the use of Professor between UK and American English, as the latter applies the title to any academic who teaches, no matter their seniority (OED Online, 'professor, n.' [Oxford University Press, June 2016], accessed 15 August 2016, www.oed.com). 87 per cent of the books published in America in our corpus feature a professor, compared to 70 per cent of those published in the UK, which will also contribute slightly to the predominance of the title Professor overall, as books published in the United States make up just over a third of the corpus. Many early examples feature a Professor as teacher, as shall be seen in Section 3.

[108] The range of terms here reflects the international nature of the corpus build, incorporating differences in institutional terminology between different English-speaking nations.

case with the bespectacled, gowned scholars seen in the background of the town square in *Zeralda's Ogre*[109]).

Standard online bibliographies, major library catalogues, specific children's literature resources and digital libraries were consulted. These included WorldCat[110] and libraries such as The British Library,[111] The National Library of Scotland,[112] The National Library of Australia[113] and The Library of Congress.[114] Specific catalogues of children's literature that were utilised include The International Children's Digital Library,[115] The International Youth Library,[116] The Children's Literature Collection at Roehampton University,[117] Children's Literature Research Collections at the University of Minnesota,[118] The National Centre for Children's Books (UK),[119] The Center for Children's Books at the University of Illinois at Urbana-Champaign,[120] The Baldwin Library of Historical Children's Literature at the University of Florida[121] and the Children's Literature Collection at the State Library of Victoria.[122] Digital libraries used included Google Books,[123] Hathi Trust Digital Library,[124] the Internet Archive[125] and the Digital Public Library of America.[126] The coverage and cataloguing in these resources varied, but the combination of a positive match

[109] T. Ungerer, *Zeralda's Ogre* (New York, NY: Harper & Row, 1967), p. 3.

[110] www.worldcat.org, a union catalogue of library content and services libraries, featuring collections from those that participate in the Online Computer Library Center (OCLC) global cooperative.

[111] www.bl.uk [112] www.nls.uk [113] www.nla.gov.au [114] www.loc.gov

[115] en.childrenslibrary.org [116] www.ijb.de/en/about-us.html

[117] http://urweb.roehampton.ac.uk/digital-collection/childrens-literature-collection/

[118] www.lib.umn.edu/clrc [119] www.sevenstories.org.uk

[120] http://ccb.lis.illinois.edu [121] http://ufdc.ufl.edu/juv

[122] www.slv.vic.gov.au/search-discover/explore-collections-theme/childrens-books

[123] https://books.google.co.uk/ [124] www.hathitrust.org

[125] https://archive.org/index.php [126] https://dp.la/

on at least one of the search terms and a note that a book was illustrated was enough to check a copy, ideally of the physical book or a digitised version from a reputable source, for an instance to be included in this corpus. In some cases, user-generated videos of children's books being read aloud, which had been posted to YouTube,[127] also proved to be a useful resource for the checking of details (although the problematic relationship of these amateur videos to official publishing channels is acknowledged).

In addition to traditional bibliographic methods, the building of the corpus was facilitated by interacting with online communities and via social media. Many of the mentions of universities, professors or doctors do not appear either in the title of the book or in library catalogue descriptions, meaning examples were not apparent through a traditional literature search: for example, Professor Euclid Bullfinch in *Danny Dunn and the Antigravity Paint*[128] or Mrs Hatchett, Doctor of Literature in *The Pirate's Mixed-Up Voyage*.[129] However, there are various other online sources that contain textual details, including listings on Amazon,[130] eBay[131] and online market-places specialising in rare books such Abe Books,[132] Alibris[133] and Biblio:[134] these are useful precisely because they contain alternative descriptions to

[127] www.youtube.com. Although useful to researchers, and promoted online as a 'free alternative to eBooks' (Healthy Family Magazine 'Kids Books on YouTube: They Are a Free Alternative to eBooks' [n. d.], available online from http://healthy-family.org/kids-books-on-youtube/), this common amateur practice is unauthorised and obviously infringes the rights of copyright holders.

[128] J. Williams and R. Abrashkin, *Danny Dunn and the Anti-Gravity Paint*, illustrated by E. J. Keats (New York, NY: McGraw Hill, 1956).

[129] M. Mahy and M. Chamberlain, *The Pirate's Mixed-Up Voyage: Dark Doings in the Thousand Islands* (London: Puffin, 1985), p. 61.

[130] www.amazon.co.uk [131] www.ebay.co.uk [132] www.abebooks.co.uk

[133] www.alibris.co.uk [134] http://biblio.co.uk/

library catalogues. In particular, user reviews on Amazon and other social media sites for reviewing, tracking and rating books, such as GoodReads,[135] LibraryThing,[136] BookDigits[137] and Shelfari,[138] and fan forums such as posts on Stack Exchange,[139] revealed university-related content. The author's own use of social media throughout this project helped identify candidates: finds were parked on a dedicated Tumblr microblog, 'Academics in Children's Picture Books',[140] and the topic was regularly discussed on the social media platform Twitter.[141] In 2014 a preliminary analysis of the corpus was presented on the author's blog,[142] which was syndicated and featured elsewhere online[143] and in print in the *Times Higher Education*.[144] This activity

[135] www.goodreads.com [136] www.librarything.com [137] http://bookdigits.com

[138] www.shelfari.com. In July 2016 this platform merged with GoodReads.

[139] For example, see the post on the Science Fiction and Fantasy Stack Exchange, 'Children's books from the 80s about a professor who used his smoking pipe to teleport himself, a girl and a boy to other worlds?' (9 May 2013), https://scifi .stackexchange.com/questions/35353/childrens-books-from-the-80s-about-a-pro fessor-who-used-his-smoking-pipe-to-tel.

[140] http://academiainchildrenspicturebooks.tumblr.com. Originally set up to just deal with pre-school literature, the project expanded to cover illustrations in all books marketed towards children.

[141] www.twitter.com/melissaterras

[142] M. Terras, 'Male, Mad and Muddle-Headed: Academics in Children's Picture Books'. Melissa Terras' Blog (2014a), http://melissaterras.org/2014/02/05/ male-mad-and-muddleheaded-academics-in-childrens-picture-books/.

[143] M. Terras, 'Male, Mad and Muddleheaded: The Portrayal of Academics in Children's Books is Shockingly Narrow.' The Impact Blog, London School of Economics (2014b), http://blogs.lse.ac.uk/impactofsocialsciences/2014/02/14/academics-in-childrens-pic ture-books/; Academia Obscura, 'The Portrayal of Academics in Kids Books – A Chat with Melissa Terras' (2015), www.academiaobscura.com/melissa-terras-interview.

[144] C. Parr, 'The Scholarly Web: Is "male, mad and muddle-headed" a fair description of the modern-day academic?', *Times Higher Education* (13 February 2014), www.time

encouraged others to get in contact to propose further candidates for inclusion: 20 per cent of the corpus was provided by readers' suggestions, which would not have been found by any other method. For example, two professors in an *Oor Wullie* cartoon,[145] spotted by Ann Gow and sent to the author via Twitter: 'Crivens, profs from Oor Wullie, 1944. A'bodys stereotype.'[146]

It is acknowledged that there will be other relevant texts that have not been found,[147] but the limits of both traditional and non-traditional bibliographic methods to gather candidates for the corpus have been exhausted.[148]

shighereducation.com/comment/opinion/the-scholarly-web-13-february-2014/2011189.article

[145] The Sunday Post, 'Oor Wulllie' (14 May 1944, p. 11), featured in Dudley Watkins (ed.), *The Broons and Oor Wullie: The Roaring Forties* (Dundee: DC Thomson, 2002).

[146] Oor Wullie ® © DC Thomson & Co. Ltd 2017. Used By Kind Permission of DC Thomson & Co. Ltd; A. Gow, Tweet, 'Crivens, profs from Oor Wullie, 1944. A'bodys stereotype' (28 April 2015), https://twitter.com/agow/status/593187045742399488.

[147] Since carrying out this analysis, five further professors have come to light: Professor Freidrich Bhaer in L.M. Alcott, *Little Women*, *Volume 2* (Boston: Roberts Brothers, 1869) also known as Good Wives; Professor Sardine in A. McCall Smith, *The Chocolate Money Mystery* (London: Bloomsbury, 2006); Professor Bunty Wilson in P. Ardagh and M. Gordon, *Egyptians* (London: Scholastic, 2009); Professor Tangle in R. Hunt and A. Brychta, *Submarine Adventure*. Oxford Reading Tree (Oxford: Oxford University Press, 2011) and Dr Schwartz in J. Brown, 'Flat Stanley: Stanley in Space' (London: Egmont, 2013). Unfortunately, it was too late to include them in the results. Yes, I wrote an Element about children's literature and missed a character from *Little Women*.

[148] It is accepted in the field of 'Data-Rich Literary History' that building a corpus is a 'critical and interpretive enterprise' which has to deal with a 'significant lack of overlap between established bibliographical records and the holdings of . . . major,

In addition, the online information environment is ever shifting and it is difficult to replicate the conditions and sources upon which a search was based: if this corpus were started in the 'now' of the reader, it would likely be different to the one on which this analysis is based, which was gathered between 2012 and 2016. The constraints of copyright upon digital libraries plays a part in the ease of finding texts, with many pre-1920s texts being available digitally in the public domain, and those after unable to be computationally full-text searched.

Paradoxically, given how useful online search mechanisms were to finding texts, it was incredibly difficult to identify *bona fide* candidates for the corpus printed after 2007, given the exponential rise in self-published ebooks. Although the '[s]elf-publishing of books has a long and illustrious history',[149] the ease at bringing self-published books to market changed in 2007 when the Kindle Digital Text Platform was launched, allowing authors to format and upload texts for sale as self-published books on Amazon.[150] 'Publishers' such as CreateSpace, iUniverse, Lulu Enterprises, Inc., Xlibris Corporation and AuthorHouse are actually print-on-demand

mass-digitized collection', meaning that corpus-based studies will only ever be inherently partial because of the patchy information environments which support their construction (Bode, 'The Equivalence of "Close" and "Distant" Reading', pp. 13–17). Some suggest that comprehensiveness should not be the goal of such corpora as they 'artificially' reify 'bodies of texts that might in fact be far more heterogeneous and unruly' (Rosen, 'Combining "Close" and "Distant"'); however, the combination of computational methods with traditional modes of literary analysis can yield new insights (ibid.).

[149] J. Dilevko and K. Dali, The self-publishing phenomenon and libraries, *Library & Information Science Research*, 28(2), (2006), pp. 208–234, p. 208.

[150] R. A. Munarriz, 'Why Kindle Will Change the World', *The Motley Fool* (27 November 2007), www.fool.com/investing/general/2007/11/27/why-kindle-will-change-the-world.aspx

services which individually print ebooks once a sale has been made, supporting the self-publishing market.[151] At the time of writing, there are over one million self-published books listed on Amazon via its CreateSpace Independent Publishing Platform service.[152]

These changes in the publishing environment have resulted in the flooding of the literature market with digital-only texts of variable quality, with little signs of readership.[153] For example, an imprint of Speedy Books LLC[154] giving itself the author name 'Baby Professor' uploaded 102 digital-only children's books for Kindle to Amazon on 15 December 2015 alone.[155] Given the huge number of ebooks of questionable quality identified by the methodology that were published after 2007, it was decided to exclude digital-only, or print-on-demand, texts from the corpus. Examples thus excluded on these grounds include the print-on-demand *Professor Woodpecker's Banana Sandwiches*[156] and the only-available-in-ebook *The Adventures of Professor*

[151] J. Bradley, B. Fulton, M. Helm and K. A. Pittner, 'Non-Traditional Book Publishing', *First Monday*, 16(8), (2011), http://journals.uic.edu/ojs/index.php/fm/article/view/3353/3030

[152] www.createspace.com/AboutUs.jsp

[153] Bradley, Fulton, Helm and Pittner, 'Non-Traditional Book Publishing'; S. Carolan and C. Evain, 'Self-Publishing: Opportunities and Threats in a New Age of Mass Culture', *Publishing Research Quarterly*, 29(4), (2013), pp. 285–300; R. McCrum, 'The BFG, Skellig, Aubrey . . . children's books boom', *The Guardian* (Sunday, 3 September 2017), https://amp.theguardian.com/books/2017/sep/02/young-readers-drive-book-sales.

[154] www.speedypublishing.co

[155] Amazon, 'Baby Professor', Author Page (2016), www.amazon.co.uk/Baby%20Professor/e/B019G317ZS

[156] H and T Imaginations Limited, *Professor Woodpecker's Banana Sandwiches* (AuthorHouse: Print on Demand, 2007).

Bumble and the Bumble Bees: the pool,[157] neither of which have been included in any of the 16,452 library collections worldwide that share their digital bibliographic catalogues via WorldCat.[158] It should be noted that the vast numbers of digital-only ebooks produced for children since 2007 raises methodological questions for the study of present-day children's literature, just as questions are being raised and methods developed within the library sector to catalogue and process self-published items and e-resources.[159]

Once candidates for inclusion were identified, the texts were consulted to check they met the criteria. More than three-quarters of the corpus was purchased. The current low cost of second-hand books, many retailing for a penny online, made this feasible.[160] Rare and prohibitively expensive texts were consulted while on other academic business to major libraries including The

[157] S. Brailovsky, *The Adventures of Professor Bumble and the Bumble Bees: The Pool* (Silverlake Ebooks, 2010).

[158] OCLC, 'Inside Worldcat' (2017), www.oclc.org/en/worldcat/inside-worldcat .html?redirect=true

[159] J. Fluvog, M. Collins, D. Hale, A. K. Pace and G. Sinclair, 'Meeting the E-Resources Challenge through Collaboration: An OCLC Perspective on Effective Management, Access, and Delivery of Electronic Collections', *The Serials Librarian*, 68(1–4) (2015), pp. 168–172; R. Holley, 'Self-Publishing and Academic Libraries', in D. M. Mueller (ed.), *Proceedings of the Association of College and Research Libraries Conference 2015*, Association of College and Research Libraries (Chicago, IL: American Library Association, 2015), pp. 706–712, www.tandfonline.com/doi/ abs/10.1080/0361526X.2015.1016857; N. Tuncer, and R., David, *The Cataloging of Self-Published Items* (Rome: International Association of Music Libraries Annual Congress, 5 July 2016), https://docs.google.com/presentation/d/ 1PMmBw8mpnp_h7GVLTkMiSJUKxTd3K2V6RLj2XEbQzmE/edit#slide=id .p4

[160] Even still, once postage is factored in, this habit incurred costs of well over £2000. For an overview of this marketplace, see C. Marsh, 'Can you really make a living by selling used books on Amazon for a penny?' (Guardian Books, 14 April 2015),

British Library, The National Library of Scotland, The Koninklijke Bibliotheek, and The National Library of Australia. Online versions of texts from digital libraries were extensively used. Digitised versions of twenty-one items were procured using 'digitisation on demand' services, mainly from libraries in North America. For example, *The Dream Slayer Mystery, Or, the Professor's Startling Crime*[161] was digitised within a matter of days, without cost, by Northern Illinois University Libraries (thanks!). Despite this multi-pronged approach, there were twenty books identified that could not be viewed in person: although Legal Deposit Libraries can request copies of all books printed within their jurisdiction, the current situation for library provision of children's book collections was explained by John Scally, the National Librarian of Scotland:

> Over the centuries that legal deposit has been in existence, children's books have not always been rigorously claimed from publishers, so that there are gaps in the record. Some of the sub-formats within children's publishing, for example foam 'bath books', wall charts, and sticker books have always been collected in a selective manner, while other format types are collected in their entirety but only by geographic region (so, for example, Scotland acquires all school workbooks relating to the Scottish curriculum). In recent decades, as there has been a wider understanding of the importance of collecting children's literature, the national libraries have worked to fill the gaps

www.theguardian.com/books/2015/apr/14/selling-used-books-on-amazon-for-a-penny.

[161] D. Dotson, *The Dream Slayer Mystery, Or, the Professor's Startling Crime* (New York, NY: Munro's Publishing House, 1900).

retrospectively and today collect texts produced for children across the full range of print and non-print materials in the same way as we collect any other type of literature, and in addition we and other libraries now have special collections of children's books which provide a rich resource for researchers.[162]

As a result, it can be difficult to find print copies of minor, pre-twentieth century children's books, even in major national libraries. The twenty potential books that could not be located, many of which were printed in Singapore and Malaysia,[163] were therefore sadly excluded from the analysis, although they are listed in Appendix C.

3.2 *Analysing the Corpus*

Once potential books had been identified, they first had to be checked to see if they met the relatively strict criteria for inclusion. Firstly, it became apparent that mentions or illustration of any facet of higher education were for the most part associated with specific fictional characters, meaning the research began to focus on these doctors and professors. Books were checked to ensure they did contain images relating to a fictional academic, keeping the analysis here strictly to fantasy: heavily illustrated books discussing the work of real academics and their research are not included. There is a parallel strand of these texts throughout the history of children's literature: for example,

---

[162] J. Scally, Personal communication: 'Checking Children's Books Collection Stats', reply to email from Melissa Terras, 17 March 2017. This statement was prepared with thanks to a variety of additional NLS staff, including Helen Vincent (Rare Books), Graeme Forbes (Collections Management), Graham Hawley (General Collections) and Graham Hogg (Rare Books).

[163] No business trip to these countries was forthcoming, alack.

Victorian texts encouraging curiosity and experimentation, such as *The Boys' Playbook of Science*[164] and *A Short History of Natural Science: And of the Progress of Discovery from the Time of the Greeks to the Present Day*.[165] More recently, there are many biographies of real scientific figures specifically produced for the children's literature market. This is a fascinating subgenre, with a variety of picturebook biographies available for leading scientific figures such as Mary Anning,[166] Albert Einstein[167] and Marie Curie.[168] For this study it was felt that comparing the representation of fictional academics such as Professor Pippy Pee-Pee Diarrheastein Poopypants Esquire[169] or *Professor PigglePoggle*[170] to the accomplishments of world-leading innovators such as Anning or Einstein was

[164] J. H. Pepper, *The Boy's Playbook of Science* (George Routledge and Sons, 1881).

[165] A. B. Buckley, *A Short History of Natural Science: And of the Progress of Discovery from the Time of the Greeks to the Present Day*, *for the Use of Schools and Young Persons* (New York, NY: D. Appleton and Company, 1910).

[166] L. Anholt and S. Moxley, *Stone Girl, Bone Girl: The Story of Mary Anning* (New York, NY: Orchard Books, 1999); C. Brighton, *The Fossil Girl: Mary Anning's Dinosaur Discovery* (Brookfield, CT: Millbrook Press, 1999); S. M. Walker and P. V. Saroff, *Mary Anning: Fossil Hunter* (Minneapolis, MN: Carolrhoda Books, 2001).

[167] D., Brown, *Odd Boy Out: Young Albert Einstein* (Boston, MA: Houghton Mifflin Co., 2004); J. M. Brallier and R. A. Parker, *Who was Albert Einstein?* (New York, NY: Grosset and Dunlap, 2002); B. Meltzer and C. Eliopoulos, *I am Albert Einstein* (New York, NY: Dial Books for Young Readers, an imprint of Penguin Group (USA) LLC, 2014).

[168] A. E. Steinke and R. Xavier, *Marie Curie and the Discovery of Radium* (New York, NY: Barron's, 1987); C. C. Miller, S. Larson and M. Heike, *Marie Curie and Radioactivity* (Mankato, MN: Capstone Press, 2007); M. Venezia, *Marie Curie: Scientist who Made Glowing Discoveries* (New York, NY: Children's Press, 2009).

[169] D. Pilkey, *Captain Underpants and the Perilous Plot of Professor Poopypants* (New York, NY: Scholastic, 1999).

[170] R. Charlton and A. Matheson, *Professor Pigglepoggle* (Dartmouth, NS: Little Fishes Publishing, 2004).

simply not appropriate. For an analysis of the portrayal of scientists in children's science biographies, see Dagher and Ford:[171] non-fiction texts are often aspirational and can exist as a counterpoint to the biases which are entrenched within fiction, and an analysis specifically of how academics are represented within these would be an obvious future study.

Generic scientists with no academic title or stated university affiliation are not included (which would be another future study). This excludes the likes of the wonderful Mrs Castle, who goes to work as an atomic scientist while her husband stays at home, minds the children and makes plum preserves in *Jam: A True Story*,[172] given there is no mention of her academic title or university setting. Medical doctors are not included in the corpus, unless they are noted as carrying out some aspect of university-based research, for example, *Dr Dog*,[173] who 'went to a Conference in Brazil to give a talk about Bone Marrow'[174], or Doc Eisenbart in *Daisy-Head Mayzie*,[175] who thinks that the plant growing out of Mayzie's head will assist him in getting research funding. Doctor Dolittle also falls into this category,[176] as he leaves medicine to undertake zoological research (although he is on the very borderline of being included in this study,

---

[171] Z. R. Dagher and D. J. Ford, 'How are scientists portrayed in children's science biographies?' *Science & Education*, 14(3–5), (2005), 377–393.

[172] M. Mahy and H. Craig, *Jam: A True Story* (Boston, MA: Atlantic Monthly Press, 1985).

[173] B. Cole, *Dr Dog* (London: Red Fox, 1994).

[174] From Cole, *Dr Dog* (p. 4), published by Jonathan Cape. Reproduced by permission of The Random House Group Ltd © 1994.

[175] Dr Seuss, *Daisy-Head Mayzie* (London: Harper Collins, 1994), p. 29.

[176] H. Lofting, *The Story of Doctor Dolittle* (New York, NY: Frederick A. Stokes Company, 1920).

showing how difficult it can be to set up exhaustive classification frameworks).

Characters that first appear in film, television or video games are excluded: this research focusses on those that originate from children's texts, rather than in book spin-offs created from other media. This eliminated a variety of material including: books containing Professor Yaffle from the much-loved television show *Bagpuss*,[177] the *Professor Fizzy* cookbooks based on the online series by PBS Kids, *Fizzy's Lunch Lab*;[178] the professors in *Pokémon Black and White*, a manga cartoon book series based on the *Pokémon* video game;[179] and the hundreds of books based around the Pixar film *Monsters University*.[180] These are just some of the academic characters found that did not have their genesis in books: an analysis of the representations of higher education in other media marketed to children is an obvious follow-up study.

Characters who appear first in magazines and comics specifically marketed towards a pre-teen audience were included – which meant that professors appearing in *Wide Awake* (1886), *St Nicholas* (1888), *The Up To Date Boy's Library* (1900), *Oor Wullie* (Sunday Post 1944), *Eagle* (1950), *Jinty* (1977), *Toby and See-saw* (1977) and *Rupert the Bear* (1993) feature. Given the importance of children's magazines and serials to the history of children's literature,[181] it seems churlish to exclude them here, and comics have been included in other

---

[177] P. Firmin and O. Postgate, *Bagpuss* (Smallfilms, BBC, 1974).

[178] D. Schlafman and E. Sussman, *Fizzy's Lunch Lab* [TV Series] (USA: CloudKid Studios, PBS Kids, 2009 onwards), http://pbskids.org/lunchlab/.

[179] H. Kusaka, S. Yamamoto, A. Roman, T. Miyaki and S. Daigle-Leach, *Pokémon Black and White: Vol. 1* (San Francisco, CA: VIZ Media, 2011) onwards.

[180] D. Scanlon, *Monsters University* [Motion Picture] (USA: Pixar, 2013).

[181] B. Alderson, 'The Making of Children's Books', in A. Immel (ed.), *The Cambridge Companion to Children's Literature* (Cambridge: Cambridge University Press, 2009), pp. 35–54, p. 42.

studies of children's literature.[182] However, because of the difficulties in finding content in early comics, it is likely that they are a source of more academics for the corpus, and this shall continue to be pursued in a future study via references in the Grand Comics Database.[183] Comics marketed towards a young-adult audience and upwards, such as superhero titles, were excluded from the analysis given the complexity of knowing whether this material is age-appropriate (although, without a doubt, many of these comic books are accessed and read by younger children[184]).

---

[182] For example, Van Gorp, Rommes and Emons, 'From the Wizard to the Doubter: Prototypes of Scientists and Engineers in Fiction and Non-Fiction Media Aimed at Dutch Children and Teenagers'. For further ongoing discussion regarding the relationship between literature and comic books, see R. Barthes and S. Heath, *Image–Music–Text* (London: Macmillan, 1978); R. Varnum and C. T. Gibbons (eds.), *The Language of Comics: Word and Image* (Jackson, MS: University Press of Mississippi, 2007); and T. Groensteen, B. Beaty and N. Nguyen, *The System of Comics* (Jackson, MS: University Press of Mississippi, 2009). J. Simons, 'Gender Roles in Children's Fiction', in M. O. Grenby and A. Immel (Eds.), *The Cambridge Companion to Children's Literature* (Cambridge: Cambridge University Press, 2009), pp. 143–158 states, 'The quality of publications like ... the *Eagle* ... was widely disparaged, but the comic book had a profound effect on the development of mainstream children's literature by popularising juvenile literary typologies including the adventure story, the school story, the science-fiction narrative, and the historical novel, all of which had already proved their appeal to boy readers in books ... and mass-market periodicals in the latter part of the nineteenth century' (p. 153).

[183] www.comics.org

[184] It is difficult to know which version of superhero comics are appropriate for a pre-teen audience, as they often appear in different versions, and in addition, many of these texts are spin-offs from other media. Our exclusion of these meant candidates such as Professor Hamilton in Scott McCloud, Rick Burchett, Jerry Siegel, Joe Shuster and DC Comics Inc., *Superman Adventures: A Big Problem* (North Mankato, MN: Stone Arch Books, 2014) do not appear in our corpus. See M. J. Von Vulte,

Books originally written for or marketed towards adults, which may now be commonly thought of as Young Adult Fiction, were also excluded (in particular, the works of Jules Verne fall into this category,[185] as do those of Arthur Conan Doyle). There are fictional reimaginings of characters that first appear in previously published fiction, with Frankenstein and Frankenstein's monster (who are often conflated) frequently reimagined as characters in other children's books; for example, *Making Friends with Frankenstein*;[186] *The Frankenstein Teacher*;[187] and *Robot Zombie Frankenstein.*[188] Given the huge volume of these, just one randomly chosen example is included here for completeness (*Dr Frankenstein's Human Body Book: The Monstrous Truth about How Your Body Works*[189]); likewise, one reimagining of Professor Van Helsing from *Dracula* (*How to Slay a Werewolf*[190]) is included. An analysis of how famous literary figures (such as Frankenstein and his monster, or Dracula and Van Helsing) have been repurposed in children's literature would be a separate study.

'Age-Appropriate Comic Books' (November 2013), www.toronto4kids.com/November-2013/Age-Appropriate-Comic-Books for an overview of the mechanisms that can be used to determine suitable readership for comic books.

[185] A. B. Evans, *Jules Verne Rediscovered: Didacticism and the Scientific Novel* (Westport, CT: Greenwood Publishing Group, 1988).

[186] Colin McNaughton, *Making Friends with Frankenstein: A Book of Monstrous Poems and Pictures* (Cambridge, MA: Candlewick Press, 1994).

[187] T. Bradman and P. Kavanagh, *The Frankenstein Teacher* (London: Corgi Pups, 1998).

[188] A. Simon, *Robot Zombie Frankenstein!* (Somerville, MA: Candlewick Press, 2012).

[189] R. Walker and N. Abadzis, *Dr Frankenstein's Human Body Book: The Monstrous Truth about How Your Body Works* (London and New York, NY: Dorling Kindersley Publishing, 2008).

[190] M. Howard and S. Walker, *How to Slay a Werewolf* (Tunbridge Wells: Ticktock, 2014).

Each academic is only counted once in the quantitative analysis, so in the case of a character who appears in multiple books in a series, such as *Professor Branestawm*,[191] they are only recorded the first time they appear in illustrated form (which may not be in the first edition of the text: for example, Professor Ptthmllnsprts appears in Kingsley's *The Water-Babies* in 1863, but is not illustrated until the 1885 edition; Dr Mary Malone appears in Pullman's *The Subtle Knife* of 1997, but is not pictured until the Folio Society Edition in 2008[192]). This concentrated the corpus on when figures were first presented to a childhood readership.[193] Illustrated books with a Professor or Doctor in the title are included even if there is not an illustration of that individual: it was noted during the course of the research that the academic can sometimes be an absent, omniscient narrator, guiding the reader through a voice of authority (although these texts are in the minority, with only five in the corpus: for example, Professor Miriam Carter in *The Mystery of Unicorns, The True History Revealed*[194]). Both fiction and non-fiction texts were examined, as fictional professors are often employed as a device of authority to encourage education and instruction in factual texts, as well as being characters in fiction:

---

[191] Hunter, *The Incredible Adventures of Professor Branestawm* 1993 onwards.

[192] Pullman, P., *His Dark Materials: Northern Lights, The Subtle Knife, The Amber Spyglass*. 3 Volume Set. Illustrated by Peter Bailey (London: Folio Society, 2008).

[193] Developing a method of fractional counting, to note when an academic appears in every book across a series, would have been an alternative and more advanced bibliometric approach; see W. Glänzel, 'The need for standards in bibliometric research and technology', *Scientometrics*, 35(2), (1996), pp. 167–176 and A. Perianes-Rodriguez, L. Waltman and N. J. van Eck, 'Constructing bibliometric networks: A comparison between full and fractional counting', *Journal of Informetrics*, 10(4), (2016), pp. 1178–1195 for an overview of this method.

[194] R. Green, E. Hawkins, R. Williams, I. Andrew, P. Brown and B. Manson, *The Mystery of Unicorns* (Dorking: Templar Publishing, 2011).

ambitiously, the full range of books produced as part of the children's literature market is considered here.

Once the corpus was constructed, all books were read and notes taken on the text. An open coded content analysis[195] was used to identify and delineate concepts about each academic, including name, gender, age, appearance, subject area, temperament, place of publication etc., using a developing coding scheme to produce label variables that emerged from the data itself as each individual instance was examined. Based on a grounded theory methodology,[196] this technique assists in the synthesis of large amounts of information[197] and can facilitate an efficient and effective summative evaluation of documentary material.[198] Previous studies have used a fixed coding instrument developed in advance of the analysis of the data: for example, Chambers[199] developed the 'Draw-a-Scientist Test' (DAST), which looked at seven common features of scientists in addition to gender, and this has been adapted and used since by others.[200] Instead, a coding instrument that could

[195] J. Corbin and A. Strauss, *Basics of Qualitative Research*. Third Edition. (Newbury Park, CA: Sage, 2008).

[196] B. G. Glaser and A. L. Strauss, *The Discovery of Grounded Theory: Strategies for Qualitative Research* (Chicago, IL: Aldine Publishers, 1967).

[197] K. Charmaz, *Constructing Grounded Theory: A Practical Guide Through Qualitative Analysis*. Introducing Qualitative Methods Series (London: Sage Publications, 2006).

[198] H. F. Hsieh and S. E. Shannon, 'Three approaches to qualitative content analysis', *Qualitative Health Research*, 15(9), (2005), pp. 1277–1288.

[199] D. W. Chambers, 'Stereotypic images of the scientist: the Draw-a-Scientist Test', *Science Education*, 67(2), (1983), 255–265.

[200] Such as W. J. Sumrall, 'Reasons for the perceived images of scientists by race and gender of students in grades 1–7', *School Science and Mathematics*, 95(2), (1995), 83–90; K. D. Finson, J. B. Beaver and B. L. Cramond, 'Development and field test of a checklist for the Draw-a-Scientist Test', *School Science and Mathematics*,

expand to encompass many aspects as the analysis progressed was employed.[201] For example, as it became clear that gender uniformity was a major issue, the gender of the writer of each text was determined (to the best available knowledge)[202] in order to ascertain whether there was a correlation between male writers and male protagonists. Working with a large but defined set of texts which did not exceed 'a single researcher's analytic capabilities'[203] meant that this coding methodology was the most efficient for this application. Data were checked and cross-referenced at various intervals, including a complete corpus check at the close of the analysis to identify any duplication or errors, allowing the results to be audited and 'validated in principle'[204] even though undertaken by a sole researcher. This analysis was undertaken incrementally from 2014 onwards, and finalised alongside the final list of texts included in 2016, with the write-up undertaken from August 2016 onwards.

Clark notes that, while quantitative approaches such as content analysis provide a valuable tool for feminist and socialist analyses of children's literature, the limits of positivist methodologies can result in narrow findings

---

95(4), (1995), 195–205; and Rawson and McCool, 'Just Like All the Other Humans?'.

[201] This follows the refinement of content analysis instruments for studying children's literature in Anderson and Hamilton, 'Gender Role Stereotyping of Parents in Children's Picture Books' and Hamilton, Anderson, Broaddus and Young, 'Gender Stereotyping and Under-Representation of Female Characters in 200 Popular Children's Picture Books'.

[202] This follows an analysis of diversity by Koss, 'Diversity in Contemporary Picturebooks', where the gender of authorship was ascertained. In our case, https://genderize.io/ was used as a classification tool.

[203] K. Krippendorff, *Content Analysis: An Introduction to its Methodology* (Sage, 2004), p. 350.

[204] Ibid., p. 39.

under a certain pressure to quantify.[205] Clark stresses the importance of qualitative methods: 'it is time for feminist social scientists to do something other than counting as well'.[206] In this study, quantitative approaches are used in tandem with detailed qualitative analysis, juxtaposing close and distant reading[207] and treating both illustrations and their surrounding stories as unified texts,[208] to provide a multifaceted approach to a broad corpus in order to identify and understand its major themes. The broad content analysis allows us to identify trends, and to track and present both individual textual and pictorial examples for closer scrutiny, looking at the 'complementarity of image and text'[209] both 'literally and expressively'.[210] This is done rather than focussing solely on illustrative techniques employed: given the size and scope of the corpus there is a full range of both monochrome and colour printing processes used, and attention is drawn to the mechanics and features of individual illustrations (given that there can be many pictures of a single character throughout even one book) only when pertinent. Examples of both illustrations and quoted text are woven into the analysis where useful and instructive, to flesh out and describe the findings. Copyright

[205] R. Clark, 'Why all the counting? Feminist social science research on children's literature', *Children's Literature in Education*, 33(4), (2002), 285–295, pp. 288–290.

[206] Ibid., p. 292. [207] Moretti, *Distant Reading*.

[208] M. O. Grenby, *Children's Literature*. Edinburgh critical guides to literature (Edinburgh University Press, 2008, this edition, 2014), p. 200.

[209] Ibid., p. 224.

[210] J. Doonan, *Looking at Pictures in Picture Books* (Woodchester: Thimble Press, 1993), p. 22.

clearance for these was an arduous and expensive process,[211] undertaken in 2017.

3.3 Conclusion

The gathering and analysis of the corpus presented here was no small task, and required a structured, methodological approach to identify texts that originated as being developed for a child reader (rather than as spin-offs from other media). Taking the time to develop such a stringent framework allows confidence in the resulting corpus of 289 books, while providing the basis for their qualitative and quantitative analysis.

4 An Analysis of Academics in Children's Illustrated Literature

An overview of the corpus is presented here, tracing the growth of appearance of academics in English language children's literature over the past 160 years, from the earliest example found until 2014. It is the academics themselves that represent the university sector: very little attention is paid to the institutions or buildings where they work. Using a mixed methods approach, their visual stereotype is explored, showing the domination of the white-haired, old, Caucasian male scientist, while textual clues identify subject area, social class and function within the plot. Academics in our corpus are revealed as loners, and intellect as strange and other, and these factors are juxtaposed with available statistics regarding the university sector, indicating a complex relationship between these stereotypes and the real-life academy.

---

[211] It required months of work, and the payment of licenses totalling £1532.90 to allow the reuse of images and quotes from in-copyright works.

4.1 An Overview of the Corpus

There were 328 academics found in 289 different English-language illustrated children's books, which are listed in Appendices A and B. The English-language corpus is international, with the majority published in the United Kingdom (49%) and the United States (41%),[212] but with texts also from Australia (5%), Canada (2%), India (1%), New Zealand (1%) and one text each from Ireland, Germany, South Africa and Singapore. It is noted that amongst these, some – such as *The Water-Babies*,[213] the *Dr Dolittle* series,[214] the *Professor Branestawm* series,[215] *The Famous Five* series,[216] *The Chronicles of Narnia*,[217] *The Moomins* series,[218] the *His Dark Materials* series[219] and the *Harry Potter* series[220] – are more popular and

[212] The British and American children's literature market is strongly interconnected; see D. C. Thacker, 'Introduction', in D. C. Thacker and J. Webb, *Introducing Children's Literature: From Romanticism to Postmodernism* (New York, NY: Routledge, 2002a), pp. 1–12, p. 8 and D. C. Thacker, 'Imagining the child', in D. C. Thacker and J. Webb, *Introducing Children's Literature: From Romanticism to Postmodernism* (New York, NY: Routledge, 2002b), pp. 13–25, p. 15).

[213] Kingsley, *The Water-Babies*. [214] Lofting, *The Story of Doctor Dolittle* onwards.

[215] Hunter, *The Incredible Adventures of Professor Branestawm* onwards.

[216] E. Blyton, *Five on a Treasure Island* (London: Hodder and Stoughton, 1942) onwards.

[217] Lewis, *The Lion, the Witch and the Wardrobe* onwards.

[218] T. Jansson, *Comet in Moominland* (London: Ernest Benn Ltd, 1951).

[219] Pullman, *Northern Lights* onwards.

[220] The *Harry Potter* series (Rowling, *Harry Potter and the Philosopher's Stone* onwards) is riddled with Professors: a title bestowed on the members of the wizarding community engaged with teaching and research and reflecting the older alignment of the term Professor with school teachers: Hogwarts School of Witchcraft and Wizardry is not a college, but 'confers the terminal degree in magic', S. Hussain 'From Indiana Jones to Minerva McGonagall, Professors See Themselves in Fiction' *The Chronicle of Higher Education* (June 9 2017) www.chronicle.com/article/From-Indiana-Jones-to-Minerva/ 240308. Although the fully illustrated editions of the Harry Potter books were not

enduring than others – such as *Walk Up! Walk Up! and See the Fools' Paradise: with the Many Wonderful Adventures There as Seen in the Strange, Surprising Peep Show of Professor Wolley Cobble*,[221] *The Wisdom of Professor Happy*,[222] *Professor Peckam's Adventures in a Drop of Water*,[223] *Professor Fred and the Fid-Fuddlephone*[224] or *Vampire Cat, the Phoney-Baloney Professor*.[225]

The books were classified given their potential audience's age range, as catalogued using the MARC 21 bibliographic specification 'target audience' 22/006/05,[226] which indicates whether a book is written for an unknown, preschool, primary, pre-adolescent or adolescent reader. No infant board books containing fictional academics were found.[227] There are ABC board books about real

published until 2015 – J. K. Rowling and J. Kay, *Harry Potter and the Philosopher's Stone*, illustrated by Jim Kay (London: Bloomsbury, 2015) – and so are outside the scope of this study, and the first editions published in the UK are non-illustrated, the original American editions published by Scholastic from 1998 contain chapter illustrations by Mary GrandPré, and it is these that are included in this analysis.

[221] *Walk Up! Walk Up! and See the Fools' Paradise: with the Many Wonderful Adventures There as Seen in the Strange Surprising Peep Show of Professor Wolley Cobble, e Raree Showman These Five and Twenty Years*. Illustrated by Wilhelm Busch (London: John Camden Hotten, 1874).

[222] C. Goldsmith, *The Wisdom of Professor Happy* (New York, NY: American Child Health Association, 1923).

[223] G. Malcolm-Smith, *Professor Peckam's Adventures in a Drop of Water* (New York, NY: Rand McNally, 1931).

[224] D. L. Pape and L. Edick Frank, *Professor Fred and the Fid-Fuddlephone* (Mankato, MN: Oddo Publishing, 1968).

[225] L. Munro Foley, *Vampire Cat: The Phoney-Baloney Professor* (New York, NY: Tom Doherty Associates, 1996).

[226] Library of Congress Network Development and MARC Standards Office, *MARC 21 Bibliographic Full 008 – Books (NR)* (Washington, DC: Library of Congress, 2015), www.loc.gov/marc/bibliographic/bd008b.html.

[227] The *Baby Einstein* series of VHS videos and other educational multimedia products targeted towards infants by Julie Aigner-Clark (1997 onwards including books, for example see J. Aigner-Clark and J. D. Marston, *Baby Shakespeare: a field trip for curious*

universities, particularly in the United States, marketed towards 'alumni, students, and toddling future graduates alike';[228] for example, *B is for Baylor*[229] and *1, 2, 3 Baylor*: 'Babies and toddlers can get to know Baylor University before they can even speak!'[230] However, no fictional academics in books for very young children were identified. Additional words have to be associated with the illustrations to indicate academic affiliation (which is a limiting prerequisite of this methodology), and in books designed to develop the vocabulary of very young children it is unlikely that the word 'Professor', or other words associated with the university, will be prioritised. Mentions of higher education which are not made in relation to a character such as a Professor or Doctor are very rare.[231] Only two exceptions to this were found: in the picturebook *Baby*

little minds into the rhythm of classic poems and the beauty of nature (Littleton, CO: Baby Einstein Press 2000)) has a bespectacled child as part of its logo, sporting Albert Einstein's particular sticking-up hair style, perpetuating an image of intelligence as geeky unkemptness to a very young audience. However, this is not a character within the books themselves, and is based on a fictionalized life phase of a real person. Aigner-Clark sold The Baby Einstein brand to Disney in 2001, who pay royalties to Corbis for the use of Einstein's likeness; see D. D'Rozario, 'The market for "Delebs" (dead celebrities): A revenue analysis', *Journal of Customer Behaviour*, 15(4), (2016), 395–414.

[228] J. H. Cook, *B is for Baylor* (Waco, TX: Baylor University Press, 2010), dust jacket.

[229] Ibid.

[230] M. Wiede, *1, 2, 3 Baylor: A Little Bear Counting Book!* Big Bear Books (Waco, TX: Baylor University Press, 2012), back cover.

[231] There are some books with a few illustrations that mention higher education but do not illustrate it. For example, university is mentioned twice in Roald Dahl's *Matilda*: Miss Honey thinks Matilda '"could be brought up to university standard in two or three years with the proper coaching." "University?" Mr Wormwood shouted, bouncing up in his chair. "Who wants to go to university, for heaven's sake! All they learn there is bad habits!" "That is not true," Miss Honey said. "If you had a heart attack this minute and had to call a doctor, that doctor would be a university graduate. If you got sued for selling someone a rotten second-hand car, you'd

Brains, the smartest baby in the world is pictured out for a walk in his buggy, pushed by his mum, and 'On the way home Baby Brains said he wanted to go to university and study medicine';[232] in *Flix*,[233] the eponymous dog goes to university, as a normal episode of the anthropomorphic life described between birth and becoming a parent himself, although there is high drama as he saves a student from a fire in the female dormitory, whom he then goes on to marry. The university setting here is incidental, although there is an unnamed, pipe-smoking dog in full academic regalia, sitting at a bench. While it would be possible to manually search through children's picture books looking for visual signifiers of higher education such as this – mortar-boards, gowns and degree scrolls – this is an impossible-to-quantify manual task.

As the target age range of audiences for the books rises, there are more instances of professors: the corpus consists of 22 % Preschool texts (ages 3–5), 33 % Primary (6–8) and 35 % Pre-adolescent (9–11) texts. Understandably, the books move more and more towards full text throughout these stages, with more contextual detail provided. Books marketed towards a 12+ (Adolescent) range make up only 10 % of the corpus, usually having small or occasional illustrated

have to get a lawyer and he'd be a university graduate too. Do not despise clever people, Mr Wormwood..."' (R. Dahl, *Matilda* (London: Jonathan Cape/Puffin Books, 1988), 1996 edition, pp. 99–100). Later, Miss Honey comments, '"I was a bright pupil . . . I could easily have got into university. But there was no question of that . . . Because I was needed at home to do the work."' (ibid., p. 199). These textual descriptions will fit into a future analysis of how academia is described in books produced for an older childhood audience. (*Matilda* © Roald Dahl and Jonathan Cape. Used by kind permission of Jonathan Cape and David Higham Agents.)

[232] S. James, *Baby Brains* (Somerville, MA: Candlewick Press, Walker Books, 2004), p. 8. Quotation copyright © 2004 Simon James. From BABY BRAINS by Simon James. Reproduced by permission of Walker Books Ltd, London SE11 5HJ. www .walker.co.uk.

[233] T. Ungerer, *Flix* (Middlesex: Roberts Rinehart Publishers, 1998), p. 19.

decorations,[234] and it can be difficult to know where the cut-off point for inclusion in the children's literature corpus is. The majority of the books are fiction (255, 88 %). There are twenty factual books (7 %) explained by a fictional professor, such as Professor Standish Brewster, professor of Pilgrimology at Plimouth University (sic), who explains the voyage of the Mayflower from Plymouth to the New World in 1620, in *Two Bad Pilgrims*,[235] or a sympathetic kingfisher who answers questions about the natural world, agony aunt style, in the *Ask Dr K. Fisher* series:

> Dear Dr. K. Fisher, I'm a rabbit and I would like to know why so many animals want to eat me . . . Dear Give Peace a Chance, The world is not a perfect place for rabbits, but nor is it for foxes and owls. . .[236]

There is one cookery book[237] and one art and craft manual.[238] Fourteen books (5 %) are a curious blend of fact and fiction: where a fictional professor explains how the world works, but get it very, very wrong. This is used for comic effect, such as in the *Dr Xargle* series[239] (this genre will be explored in Section 5), but also to persuade children of the veracity of ideas: seemingly 'academic'

---

[234] For example, Lord Asriel is illustrated in the original edition of Northern Lights only with a drawing of his hand, which features at the start of a chapter as an opening miniature vignette (Pullman, *Northern Lights*, p. 18). Professors and doctors appear regularly in text-only Young Adult Fiction, and analysing these would make an obvious follow-on study.

[235] K. Lasky and J. Manders, *Two Bad Pilgrims* (New York, NY: Viking, 2009).

[236] C. Llewellyn, *Ask Dr K. Fisher about Animals* (London: Kingfisher, Macmillan Children's Books, 2007), p. 24.

[237] L. Brash, *Professor Cook's Mind-Blowing Bakes* (London: Wayland, Hachette Children's Books, 2012).

[238] N. Cameron, *How to Make Awesome Comics: With Professor Panels and Art Monkey* (Oxford: David Fickling Books, 2014).

[239] J. Willis and T. Ross, *Dr Xargle's Book of Earthlets* (London: Andersen Press, 1988) onwards.

expertise is used to promote creationism and other religious propaganda, for example in *Professor Noah Thingertoo's Bible Fact Book, Old Testament.*[240]

4.2 The Appearance of Professors in Children's Literature

The earliest Professor is to be found in a chapbook primer,[241] printed circa 1850:[242] *The Parents' Best Gift: A New Spelling Book, Containing a Large*

---

[240] C. Gray, *Professor Noah Thingertoo's Bible Fact Book: Old Testament* (Wheaton, IL: Victor Books, 1996).

[241] Readers wondering why The Academy of Lagado and its scholars and professors, featured in the third part of J. Swift, *Travels into Several Remote Nations of the World: In Four Parts. By Lemuel Gulliver, First a Surgeon, and Then a Captain of Several Ships* (Dublin: Printed by and for J. Hyde, Bookseller in Dame's Street, 1726) – known more commonly as *Gulliver's Travels* – is not presented as the first example should note that *Gulliver's Travels* was not written as a text for children. Although the first section, regarding Lilliput, has been bowdlerised and adapted as a children's story in itself, the Academy of Lagado appears in a later part of the book and is one of the most biting parts of the satire, written for an adult audience. The same is true of the many books by Jules Verne that portray academic researchers and explorers, most famously Professor Arronax in J. Verne, *20,000 Leagues under the Sea* (London: Sampson Low, Marston, Searle, and Rivington, 1872a) and Professor Von Hardwigg (in the original French, Professor Otto Lidenbrock) in J. Verne, *A Journey to the Centre of the Earth* (London: Griffin and Farran, 1872b). Although perceived as writing for an adult audience in their original texts, the adapted and heavily edited English language translations are now commonly viewed as Young Adult Fiction. As a result, Verne's texts have been excluded from our analysis, although his influence is later noted. Arthur Conan Doyle, *The Lost World: Being an Account of the Recent Amazing Adventures of Professor George E. Challenger, Lord John Roxton, Professor Summerlee, and Mr E. D. Malone of the Daily Gazette* (London: Hodder and Stoughton, 1912), which contains Professor George E. Challenger and Professor Summerlee, does not appear in our corpus for the same reason.

[242] Although the chapbook is undated, the publisher, Ryle and Co., of Seven Dials, was operational in London between 1846–59 (British Book Trade Index, 'Details for

Quantity of Reading, Spelling, etc. with the additional cover title *Professor Howard's First Step to Learning*. The content of the primer – as is common for chapbooks – is adapted, reprinted and copied from earlier publications promoting both the Anglican Church catechisms and rote learning of letters and numbers.[243] The fictional Professor Howard featured within a classroom setting (See Figure 1) is presumably invoked to represent intellectual, academic and social authority as a positioning device to promote and encourage children's learning

RYLE & CO., London' [n. d.], http://bbti.bodleian.ox.ac.uk/details/?traderid=95849).

[243] Recycled text within the chapbook can be traced through the copying and reprinting of catechisms from Church of England, *The Book of Common Prayer and Administration of the Sacraments, and Other Rites and Ceremonies of the Church of England: With the Psalter or Psalmes of David* (1662) for a childhood audience in J. Ritson, *The Parent's Best Gift: Being a Choice Collection of Several Remarkable Examples of God's Judgments and Mercies : To which is Added, The Child's Manual; or, The Church Catechism : With Prayers for Every Day in the Week* (London: Printed and sold in Aldermary Church-Yard, London, 1750); *The Parent's Best Gift Containing the Church Catechism with Many Questions and Answers Out of the Holy Scriptures* (New York, NY: Printed by J. Harrisson, for all good children – price six pence, 1796); and Marsden, *The Parent's Best Gift: Containing the Church Catechism: Together with Divine Questions and Answers Out of the Holy Scriptures : Also Proper Directions for the Behaviour of Children towards God, their Parents, Teachers, &c.* (Colchester: Marsden, 1802). In 1845 this common title to describe the catechisms is married with the school classroom and a reading primer in Johnson, *The Parents' Best Gift for a Good Child* (London: *W. S. Johnson*, 1845). Our chapbook with Professor Howard reprints selections from these earlier texts, adding elements of G. Nicholson, *The English Primer, Or, Child's First Book* (Stourport: Printed and published by G. Nicholson, 1807), and draws heavily on 'Maxims and Proverbs' from L. Cobb, *The Treasury of Knowledge and Library of Reference* (New York, NY: Conner and Cooke, 1832), p. 445. The text was later reprinted in 1860 by W. S. Fortey, who inherited Ryle and Co.: the only difference being the change of publisher and address: *Professor Howard's First Step to Learning* (London: Fortey, 1860).

(although that authority is directed towards the adult purchasing the book: *this* primer, in an increasingly crowded market, is the one you should trust). The picture of Professor Howard with his class – reminding us that professors are associated with teaching as well as expertise – is juxtaposed with an ambiguous image on the title page that looks remarkably like Field Marshal Arthur Wellesley, the 1st Duke of Wellington (1769–1852). It was common for woodcuts to be reused by early printers,[244] and often 'children's books were built up out of woodcuts lying around in the shop or borrowed from other works'.[245] This particular untitled image is further used to convey power: it may or may not be our Professor Howard, but this is a book confidently espousing its teaching credentials in a display of male authority and privilege. There is no further mention of the professor within the text, which is a short, fourteen-page pamphlet containing the popular Tom Thumb's Alphabet,[246] reading lessons, church catechisms, and 'one hundred moral maxims' such as 'Books alone can never teach the use of books'.[247]

   The use of a Professor in the publication of this fourteen-page pamphlet in the mid-nineteenth century is significant. During this period, children's education was rapidly changing, becoming more institutionalised with an expansion of the

[244] J. Burant, 'The visual world in the Victorian age', *Archivaria*, 1(19), (1984), pp. 110–121.

[245] S. Lerer, *Children's Literature: A Reader's History, from Aesop to Harry Potter* (Chicago, IL: University of Chicago Press, 2008), p. 322.

[246] A traditional nursery rhyme in rhyming couplets which dates back to the mid-eighteenth century, beginning 'A was an archer, and shot at a frog' and ending 'Z was a Zany, a silly old fool'; see P. Crain, *The Story of A: The Alphabetization of America from The New England Primer to The Scarlet Letter* (Stanford University Press, 2000), pp. 65–72 for its printing – and reprinting – history.

[247] *The Parents' Best Gift: A New Spelling Book, Containing a Large Quantity of Reading, Spelling, etc. Professor Howard's First Step to Learning* (London: Ryle and Co., 1850). p. 13.

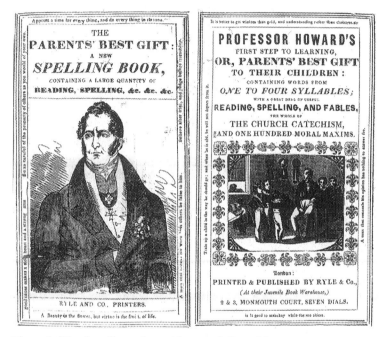

Figure 1 Woodcut illustrations, title page (left) and frontispiece (right) from *The Parents' Best Gift: Professor Howard's First Step to Learning* (circa 1850), used with permission, Bodleian Libraries, University of Oxford, Opie G 255.

scholastic system (which is reflected in children's literature of the period[248]). The new importance of learning resulted in an expanding market for ABC books,

---

[248] See F. Lawrence, 'Textbooks', in W. Lamont (ed.), *The Realities of Teaching History* (Ghatto & Windus for Sussex University Press, 1972), pp. 110–143 and E. Gargano, *Reading Victorian Schoolrooms: Childhood and Education in Nineteenth-Century Fiction* (London: Routledge, 2013).

chapbooks and primers,[249] although many of these were 'numbingly dull compilations of facts and dates which Victorian schoolchildren had to learn by heart in those "catechetical" classes'.[250] Well-circulating textbooks were printed throughout the nineteenth century that traded on the academic qualifications of the authors as an imprimatur. An 1816 guide for Young Ladies[251] contains a 'hypothetical bookseller's bill' as a 'revealing index of what were considered desirable reading habits':[252] out of twenty-four (real) texts, three are written by those with higher degrees, and sold as such: *Dr Watts' Improvement of the Mind* (first published 1741, with many subsequent editions);[253] *Essays on Rhetoric by Dr Blair* (first published in 1784 with many subsequent reprints)[254] and *Dr Mavor's New Speaker, or English Class Book (1811)*.[255] Dr Isaac Watts and Dr Hugh Blair both spent considerable time in the academy and gained

[249] Crain, *The Story of A.*

[250] M. Bentley, 'The evolution and dissemination of historical knowledge', in M. Daunton, (ed.), *The Organisation of Knowledge in Victorian Britain* (Oxford: Oxford University Press, 2005), pp. 173–198, p. 188.

[251] J. Greig, *The Young Ladies' New Guide to Arithmetic: Being a Short and Useful Selection, Containing, Besides the Common and Necessary Rules, the Application of Each Rule, by a Variety of Practical Questions, Chiefly on Domestic Affairs : Together with the Method of Making Out Bills of Parcels, Book Debts, Receipts, &c. &c. : For the Use of Ladies' Schools, and Private Teachers* (London: Baldwin, Cradock, and Joy by assignment of B. and R. Crosby, 1816), p. 15.

[252] T. L. Broughton and R. Symes, *The Governess: An Anthology* (Thrupp: Sutton Publishing, 1997), p. 61.

[253] I. Watts, *The Improvement of the Mind: or, A Supplement to the Art of Logick* (London: James Brackstone, 1741).

[254] H., Blair, *Essays on Rhetoric* (London: J. Murray, 1784).

[255] W. F. Mavor, *The New Speaker; or, English Class Book* (London: printed for B. Crosby [and others], 1811).

qualifications.[256] However, Dr Mavor is a pseudonym for Sir Richard Phillips, a schoolteacher and bookseller, and the title is presumably used for marketing purposes.[257] This established mechanism of academic titles being used to frame a text's trustworthiness crosses over into a recommendation from a fictional professor in our mid-nineteenth century chapbook: indeed, much of the religious text for this chapbook appeared in an earlier format which was promoted by an actual academic figure, Dr William Paley:[258] *Parents Best Gift containing the Church Catechism, Questions and Answers out of the Holy Scriptures. Dr Paley's Important Truths and Duties of Christianity*.[259] This title, and the habit of using an academic imprimatur to promote texts, indicates a potential trajectory for the switch into fictional endorsement of the reprint of the text in *Professor Howard's First Step to Learning*, around 1850. By the late nineteenth century, other authors with professorial titles are selling textbooks, such as *Professor Miekeljohn's Series*, one of the first, best-selling standard set of school textbooks in the late Victorian era, written by J. M. D Meikeljohn, Professor of the Theory, History, and Practice of Education at the University of St Andrews and published by Blackwoods from 1883 onwards.[260]

---

[256] J. A. Jones (ed.), *Bunhill Memorials: Sacred Reminisce nces of Three Hundred Ministers and Other Persons of Note, Who are Buried in Bunhill Fields, of Every Denomination* (London: James Paul, 1849), pp. 298–304; L. Stephen, 'Blair, Hugh', in L. Stephen, *Dictionary of National Biography*, 05 (London: Smith, Elder & Co., 1886), pp. 160–161.

[257] L. Paul, *The Children's Book Business: Lessons from the Long Eighteenth Century* (London: Routledge, 2010).

[258] Cambridge Alumni Database, William Paley 1743–1805, n. d.

[259] W. Paley, *The Parents' Best Gift. Containing the Church Catechism, Questions and Answers out of the Holy Scriptures, Dr. Paley's Important Truths and Duties of Christianity, etc.* (Chester: Printed by J. Fletcher, 1811).

[260] N. Graves, 'John Miller Dow Meiklejohn: educationist and prolific textbook author', *Paradigm*, 2(8), October 2004; N. Graves, *J. M. D. Meiklejohn: Prolific Textbook Author* (Surrey: The Textbook Colloquium, 2008).

Professors would have become more visible during this period, as the university sector was also transforming, becoming more established throughout the world and playing an increasing role in society, integrating science into a curriculum that had previously eschewed it.[261] Between the 1860s and 1930s 'a small, homogenous, elite and pre-professional university turned into a large, diversified, middle-class and professional system of higher learning',-[262] transforming universities from what had been previously been viewed as an optional phase in the development of privileged young white gentlemen into a core institution informing modern society.[263] Moving away from their 'traditional task of serving the older landed and professional elite',[264] universities started to adapt to the needs of industrial society. As 'pressure intensified on parents to invest in education',[265] and as the university curriculum became more distinct from secondary schooling, accelerated further by state intervention, we see the forming of an 'academic profession, which only becomes recognizable as such at the end of the nineteenth century'.[266] The emergence of 'the academic' expert in both research and teaching is itself part of the rise of Professionalism during the Victorian period.[267]

---

[261] J. Axtell, *Wisdom's Workshop: The Rise of the Modern University* (Princeton, NJ: Princeton University Press, 2016).

[262] K. H. Jarausch, *The Transformation of Higher Learning: Expansion, Diversification, Social Opening and Professionalization in England, Germany, Russia and the United States* (University of Chicago Press, 1983).

[263] H. Perkin, *The Origins of Modern English Society* (Routledge, 2003).

[264] R. D. Anderson, *Universities and Elites in Britain since 1800* (Vol. 16, New Studies in Economic and Social History) (Cambridge: Cambridge University Press, 1995), p. 1.

[265] Ibid., p. 7. [266] Ibid., p. 47.

[267] Perkin, *The Origins of Modern English Society*. A history of the growth of the university sector worldwide, and the nuances between different countries and

These developments in the university sector, and the growing public perception of academia as a profession, can be coupled with the fact that the nineteenth century was a period where more and more books were being created for a childhood audience, particularly in the United Kingdom and the United States: 'The latter half of the nineteenth century saw the beginnings of a great age of children's fiction, an outpouring of literature written by middle-class adults for middle-class children'.[268] In addition, advancement in printing technology at this time allowed illustrations of higher quality to be produced more easily.[269] In many ways, the confluence of these factors mean we could only expect an academic to appear fully illustrated in children's literature from the mid-nineteenth century.

There are forty-one other academics which appear in the corpus in the nineteenth century, all in its last thirty years, with twenty others from the United Kingdom and twenty-one from the United States (see Appendix B, and also the open access anthology which draws together many of these short stories and poems[270]). It should also be noted, however, that the coverage of books from the United States is influenced by the number of texts appearing in the corpus from the wonderful Baldwin Library of Historical Children's Literature at the University of Florida, which provides much digitised children's literature in the public domain: showing how mass digitisation, combined with the constraints of copyright (American texts published in or after

continents, can be found in Axtell, *Wisdom's Workshop: The Rise of the Modern University*.

[268] A. S. MacLeod, *American Childhood: Essays on Children's Literature of the Nineteenth and Twentieth Centuries* (University of Georgia Press, 1995), p. 13.

[269] E. O'Sullivan, *Historical Dictionary of Children's Literature*. Historical Dictionaries of Literature and the Arts, No. 46 (Plymouth: Scarecrow Press, 2010), p. 134.

[270] Terras, *The Professor in Children's Literature: An Anthology*.

1923 remain in copyright and generally are not digitised and made freely available, but those published prior to that can be without risk, meaning only earlier texts are freely available), can influence the dynamics of corpus-based analysis.

The appearance of professors in children's literature over this period reflects the growing importance of universities at that time in these contexts, although few characters have anything to do with academic institutions. The Professor in *The Professor's Merry Christmas*[271] is the first to be included in fiction,[272] in a Christian retelling of Dickens' *A Christmas Carol*[273] two children are illustrated delivering food to a poor, elderly professor who has decided not to celebrate Christmas, until shown visions of families, charity and the second coming. There is a showman (Professor Wolley Cobble, in *Walk Up! Walk Up!* 1874), American coming-of-age tales of hard-working students and young professionals (*Herbert Carter's Legacy, or, The Inventor's Son*,[274] *Professor Johnny*,[275] *Professor Pin*[276] and a thrilling adventure in the *The Professor's Last Skate*,[277] where a teacher recalls to his students the last time he went skating alone, years ago: breaking his leg and having to haul himself miles home across the ice). Many of the early professor's in the corpus are indistinguishable from higher-level school

[271] M. S. Clark, *The Professor's Merry Christmas* (London: SPCK, 1871).

[272] As noted previously, Professor Ptthmllnsprts appears in Kingsley, *The Water-Babies* in 1863, but is not illustrated until the 1885 edition.

[273] C. Dickens, *A Christmas Carol. In Prose. Being a Ghost Story of Christmas*. (London: Chapman and Hall 1843).

[274] H. Alger, *Herbert Carter's Legacy, or, The Inventor's Son* (Boston, MA: Loring, 1875).

[275] J. A. K., Thomas Y. Crowell Company and Rand, Avery & Co., *Professor Johnny* (New York, NY: Thomas Y. Crowell & Co., 1887).

[276] F. Lee, *Professor Pin* (Boston, MA: Pilgrim Press, 1899).

[277] J. M. Oxley, 'The Professor's Last Skate', *Wide Awake* 22(6), (May 1886), 339–342.

teachers, showing both the changing linguistic use of the term and also the formalisation of academic training: for example, the Old Professor in the *Princess of Hearts*,[278] draughted in unsuccessfully to deal with a precocious royal child. More random stories do start to appear: the grotesque Professor Menu is a 'celebrated experimental cook, who had been driven away from London because of the effect of his awful experiments on the digestions of the customers at his restaurant!',[279] discovered on an island by starving shipwrecked sailors, but whose worrying scientific experiments on food drive the narrator ambiguously to madness, or a confession, it was all a tall tale.

An early colour illustration (Figure 2)[280] appears in the fairy tale *Professor Bumphead*,[281] which publishes a lecture given by the fairy professor, on the setting up of a Society for the Prevention of Cruelty to Inanimate Objects (stressing the ridiculousness of professorial advice, at this early stage, mocking Victorian scholarly and scientific societies): 'A few well-chosen words addressed to a gate-post, flower-pot, bottle or any other inanimate object, will

---

[278] S. Braine and A. B. Woodward, *The Princess of Hearts* (Chicago, IL: Jamieson Higgins Co., 1899).

[279] J. F. Sullivan, *The Flame-Flower, and Other Stories* (London: J. M. Dent & Co., 1896), p. 203.

[280] This is a colour-offset lithograph, which was a relatively new technique at the time: see G. W. R. Ward, *The Grove Encyclopedia of Materials and Techniques in Art* (Oxford: Oxford University Press, 2008), p. 349. There is also a colour illustration of a Professor Goggles, taxidermist, in P. Newell, *Topsys and Turvys* (New York, NY: The Century Co., 1893), but there is no story associated with him, just a visual puzzle where one way up it looks like an owl, the other way, a mad professor. 'Professor Goggles taxidermist, certainly looks grim: He's just been told his last stuffed Owl does much resemble him' (p. 19).

[281] C. S. Johns, *The Fairies' Annual* (London: John Lane, 1905).

PROFESSOR BUMPHEAD

Figure 2 Professor Bumphead lecture tells us how miserable windmills are. In *The Fairies' Annual* (Johns, *The Fairies' Annual*, p. 31). Every effort has been made to trace any right-holder who may own the rights to this work (the estate of Cecil Starr Johns, and The Bodley Head), although it is believed to be in the public domain: any further information is most welcome in order to remedy permissions in future editions.

cheer its heart and encourage it to get through the terrible monotony of its existence'.[282]

Early professors in children's literature cover a range of tales and genres, symptomatic of the first one hundred years of the corpus, where there are sixty-eight academics found (thirty-eight being from the United Kingdom, with thirty from the United States). There is a warning tale of a conman and magician (Professor De Lara),[283] advice on healthy living (*The Wisdom of Professor Happy*),[284] a scientific quest in *Professor Peckam's Adventures in a Drop of Water*,[285] and an anthropomorphic short story in the style of Beatrix Potter (*Professor Porky the Porcupine*).[286] The most enduring characters of this period are the scientist Professor Ptthmllnsprts in Kingsley, *The Water-Babies*, the doctor turned zoologist *Doctor Dolittle*,[287] and the baffled scientist and inventor *Professor Branestawm*,[288] giving three best-selling blueprints for scholarly conduct in children's literature. There are two spikes Chart 1, which shows the date of publication of books in the corpus: the first towards the end of the nineteenth century shows both the growing awareness of the university sector and also the effect of full text search in public domain mass digitisation on the process of corpus building. Instances fall away once manual searching of print takes over in early twentieth-century texts, before rising again. It is only from the

[282] Ibid., p. 32.

[283] E. Nesbit, 'The twopenny spell', in E. Nesbit, *Oswald Bastable and Others* (London: Wells Gardner, Darton & Co., 1905), pp. 167–180. Obtained from https://archive .org/details/in.ernet.dli.2015.102048.

[284] Goldsmith, *The Wisdom of Professor Happy*.

[285] Malcolm-Smith, *Professor Peckam's Adventures in a Drop of Water*.

[286] H. Heaton, *Professor Porky* illustrated by H. E. M. Sellen (London: Faber and Faber, 1940).

[287] Lofting, *The Story of Doctor Dolittle*.

[288] Hunter, *The Incredible Adventures of Professor Branestawm*.

mid-twentieth century that academics in children's books gain in popularity in this dataset, becoming more prevalent (or, at least, easier to find) and settling down into established stereotypes.

It is tempting to relate the growth of the number of illustrations of academics found in children's books per year across in the second part of the twentieth century to the rapid expansion of and increased access to higher education throughout the English-speaking world within that period.[289] For example, in the United Kingdom, the number of universities more than doubled in the latter half of the twentieth century, and the population's 'overall participation in higher education increased from 3.4% in 1950, to 8.4% in 1970, 19.3% in 1990 and 33% in 2000'.[290] However, the growth shown in Chart 1 does not necessarily correlate to this; nor does it mean that academics are becoming more important as a theme in children's literature and appearing in a higher percentage of texts.

The growth in the corpus can be plotted against known data on book production from two library catalogue sources. Firstly, counts of all books catalogued as English language for a junior audience in WorldCat were manually scraped from the site.[291] Given it is so difficult to ascertain reliable statistics for book publications over time,[292] WorldCat remains a useful resource for

---

[289] Anderson, *Universities and Elites in Britain since 1800*; E. Schofer and J. W. Meyer, 'The worldwide expansion of higher education in the twentieth century', *American Sociological Review*, 70(6), (2005), pp. 898–920; Axtell, *Wisdom's Workshop: The Rise of the Modern University*.

[290] P. Bolton, 'Education: Historical Statistics', Social and General Statistics, House of Commons Library (November 2012), http://researchbriefings.files.parliament.uk/documents/SN04252/SN04252.pdf, p. 14.

[291] www.worldcat.org

[292] A. Welsh, 'Historical bibliography in the digital world', in C. Warwick, M. Terras and J. Nyhan (eds.), *Digital Humanities in Practice* (London: Facet, 2012), pp. 139–165.

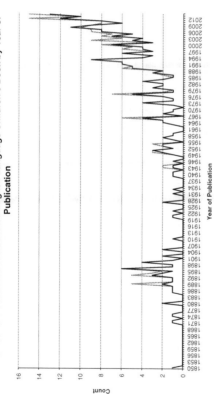

Chart 1 Academics appearing in English language children's books per year since 1850. Note, in some books, more than one academic may be featured: therefore the number of books in which they appear per year has been noted, as well as the total number of academics found per year.

quantitative analysis despite its known limitations.[293] There are 1781 books in WorldCat that were catalogued as being English-language juvenile-audience text published in 1856, 1574 in 1906, 8082 in 1956 and 50,477 in 2006 (concluding the period prior to the exponential growth of self-published books, many of which do not feature in library catalogues). Secondly, The British National Bibliography (BNB),[294] which has been recording the publishing activity of the United Kingdom and the Republic of Ireland since 1950,[295] was contacted and asked for a list of children's books published in the United Kingdom, which had been included in the BNB since its inception, and which they began cataloguing in 1961 given changing cataloguing conventions.[296] However, it should be noted that the division between children's and adult books is not often clear within the catalogue,[297] and there is yet to be a special edition of the BNB listing only children's books, given books *for* children and books *about* children are often hard to distinguish within the 'juvenile literature' heading (this is an area ripe for community input, to crowdsource a national bibliography of children's fiction and non-fiction literature). There are currently 1033 juvenile literature books in the BNB catalogued as being published in 1970, 2912 in 1980, 3653 in 1990, and 8938 in 2000. To allow comparison between

---

[293] A. H. Perrault, Global Collective Resources: A Study of Monographic Bibliographic Records in WorldCat. Online Computer Library Center (OCLC), (2002), www .oclc.org/research/grants/reports/perrault/intro.pdf; A. H. Turner, 'OCLC WorldCat as a cooperative catalog', *Cataloging & Classification Quarterly*, 48(2–3), (2010), pp. 271–278; A. Sneary, 'Moving towards data-driven development: WorldCat Collection Analysis', *Against the Grain*, 18(5), (2013), p. 12.

[294] www.bl.uk/bibliographic/natbib.html, which can also be searched at http:// bnb.bl.uk/.

[295] A. Stephens, *The History of the British National Bibliography 1950–1973* (London: British Library, 1994).

[296] Ibid., p. 8.

[297] S. G. Ray, '(5) United Kingdom', *International Library Review*, 6(3), (1974), pp. 281–284.

WorldCat and the BNB data, the volume of books catalogued as juvenile literature published per year is expressed as a percentage of the total books in each individual series, indicating that more books are produced towards the end than the middle of the twentieth century.

Chart 2 shows growth in the number of children's books appearing in the BNB and in WorldCat, year on year, from the mid-twentieth century: more books classified as juvenile literature are produced yearly. The WorldCat data (from 1850) comprises of over 1.6 million books, the BNB data (from 1961, where books published in England and Ireland were first catalogued as Children's Literature in the BNB) contains just short of 270,000 records (although there may be some false positives in this dataset, with books for children as subject being conflated with books for children as audience, so further cleaning and statistical work is needed on this dataset). Our corpus of 289 books in comparison shows a much more volatile trajectory, being more sensitive to the addition of one or two texts per year. However, all show upward trends, indicating that despite the growth of the university sector, the increase in the number of academics is correlated with the fact there are simply more and more children's books being produced in the second half of the twentieth century, rather than the topic becoming more important and prevalent in juvenile literature over time (which would be represented by curve that deviated further from the BNB and WorldCat series in Chart 2). The percentage of texts which feature an illustration of an academic (calculated by the total books per year, and the books catalogued, as above, in WorldCat or the BNB – provided all possible examples have been found, which is rather unlikely!) is roughly constant. Using the BNB introduces interesting methodological opportunities for the study of children's literature (or 'juvenile literature', as it is described as a topic in the Library of Congress Subject Headings used by the BNB) but requires a robust methodology to be developed to mitigate against statistical uncertainty. The BNB and other national

Picture-Book Professors

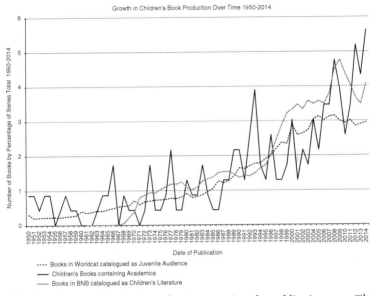

Chart 2 The growth in book production over time, by publication year. The number of children's books published that contain professors is compared to two available data sources: total number of books catalogued for juvenile audience in WorldCat, and books catalogued as 'juvenile literature' in the British National Bibliography. The x-axis represents the percentage of books published in that one year, in comparison to the total number of books published for that series between 1950 and 2014 (the series total reaches 100 %, so in the case of WorldCat we can see that 0.5 % of books classified as juvenile literature in WorldCat are published in 1950, but 3 % in 2004: the number of children's books produced over time rises year on year). In all three series, proportionally more books appear across the end of the twentieth century, suggesting that there are more children's books being published in total (which, in addition, are more likely to be catalogued in the modern library environment; see quote from Scally in Section 3.1), not that academics in children's literature are becoming proportionally more prevalent.

bibliographies[298] are, as yet, an untapped dataset for children's literature scholarship, and hold future potential for evidence-based quantitative research on the topic, provided the datasets can be further cleaned and moderated in a way which would establish them as authoritative data sources for children's book publishing.

The increase in number of books in the corpus towards the close of the twentieth century does mean that 50 per cent of the academics first appear in books published from 1993 onwards, and will therefore reflect modern representations of academia, once tropes have had a chance to develop, in a form which 'declares its debt to postmodern modes of production' with 'the rise of the experimental, multi-voiced, metafictional children's text in the latter half of the twentieth century'.[299] The prominence of academics in enduring and popular best-selling children's texts means that their influence goes far beyond this relatively low occurrence in the pantheon of children's literature, with 'famous' academics in children's literature both building and reinforcing the stereotypes used by subsequent authors and illustrators as blueprints and shorthand for their characters. Overall, distinct themes emerge which become constant: universities as places or institutions are not as important as the people within them, and fictional academics have stereotypes that emerge involving gender, race, class, age, appearance and academic subject. These – and the dominant stereotypes that emerge – will be explored and placed into context via

[298] The Library of Congress has recently made 25 million records in its online catalogue available for bulk download and analysis: see Library of Congress, 'Library offers largest release of digital catalog records in history: 25 million free records of bibliographic metadata', News from the Library of Congress, 16 May 2017, www .loc.gov/item/prn-17-068/library-offers-largest-release-of-digital-catalog-records-in-history/2017-05-16/.

[299] D. C. Thacker, 'Victorianism, empire and the paternal voice', in D. C. Thacker and J. Webb, *Introducing Children's Literature: From Romanticism to Postmodernism* (New York, NY: Routledge, 2002d), pp. 41–55, p. 141.

their external influences. Drawing on trends and stereotypes that came before them in often 'playful subversion',[300] as the stereotype of the mad male muddle-head coalesces, it can become both easier to drop a character into a children's story without need for explanation as part of intertextual exploration, and harder for writers and illustrators to confront and break free from these expected mores.

4.3 The Presence and Absence of the University

It may be thought obvious to look first at how universities are pictured as settings in children's literature. However, after reading and analysing the corpus, it became clear that any analysis should concentrate on the individuals that appear in the books, both as protagonists and minor characters, rather than the representation of universities as places or institutions: there is so very little comment on anything other than the people in the texts, either in text or as background setting in illustrations. This is unlike school stories, where 'the school features almost as a character itself',[301] or the analysis of universities in American superhero comics where the leafy green park life spaces of campus 'connect with and bolster public imaginings of U.S. institutions of higher education'.[302]

---

[300] Ibid. [301] Grenby, *Children's Literature*, p. 87.

[302] Reynolds, 'Do You Want Me to Become a Social Piranha?', p. 6. An American series for children does carry on this campus obsession: the series of sixteen Innerstar University books that accompany the American Girl branded dolls, which are spin-offs from an accompanying online virtual world (and therefore excluded from our corpus); see E. Falligant, *Braving the Lake*. Innerstar University, American Girl. (Middleton, WI: Arcana Studios, 2010). They feature maps and a complex campus design including the obviously essential Shopping Square, the Rising Star Stables, Boathouse and Library; see American Girl Wiki, Innerstar University (2015), http://americangirl.wikia.com/wiki/Innerstar_University. It took a virtual world tie-in to scope this geography out, as most university settings in our corpus are presented without explanation or situation.

There are only three books for a young audience that are mainly based in university settings, although descriptions of these are slight and show the dominance of Oxbridge and the Ivy League in popular conception of universities. *Sylvie and Bruno* and *Sylvie and Bruno Concluded* (the last novels written by Lewis Carroll, in 1889 and 1893) proceed in a rather disjointed dual setting: the university and fairyland.[303] They have a range of characters typically found around Oxbridge colleges (although no specific geographical setting is given), with seven illustrated: the Professor, the Other Professor, the Vice-Warden, the Chancellor (1889), two Heads of College, and a student (1893). The stories focus on and ridicule the people and processes within academic institutions, rather than the physical university itself: although there are mention of libraries, college halls, lecture rooms and gardens which have conversations, teaching and meetings within them, they are not described at all, and only appear as the odd brick wall or corner of a room in illustrations. There are parallels drawn between fairyland and the university system, poking fun at intellectual expertise, within the text. Much fun is made of the pursuit of funding: a visiting academic tells the tale of how professors motivated students by offering them money for correct answers, until the students made more money than the professors earn. Students were chosen by 'Scholarship Hunts' where principals chased them through the streets as they get off the train, aiming to catch the best ones (Figure 3).[304] Throughout the book, it is these characters, and their reminiscing and actions, rather than the setting, which is important.

Likewise, *Jack Dawe Super Scientist and the Professors*,[305] a book which never had a wide circulation – written by an anonymous Oxford professor for

---

[303] Carroll, L., *Sylvie and Bruno*, illustrated by Harry Furniss (London: Macmillan and Co., 1889); Carroll, L., *Sylvie and Bruno Concluded*, illustrated by Harry Furniss (London: Macmillan and Co., 1893).

[304] Carroll, *Sylvie and Bruno Concluded*, p. 188.

[305] Uncle B and Brian Green, *Jack Dawe Super Scientist and the Professors. Bedtime Stories for Technically Inclined Little Ones* (London: Allday Limited, 1964).

Figure 3 Heads of college chasing good students, in a 'cub-hunt', in Carroll, *Sylvie and Bruno Concluded* (p.189), illustrated by Harry Furniss. Public Domain: image from copy held at University of California Libraries and available at archive.org. This style of illustrating the university of Sylvie and Bruno is common throughout the text, with hints of stonework and flagstones.

his nieces and nephews – has illustrations of indistinguishable packs of male dons wearing *sub fusc* mortar boards and gowns, but little comment on the university itself. The scientist Jack Dawe works at Oxford, but is called away to deal with infestations at the Australian University, university business at The University of the Ganges, and the Congo University, and to procure computers for universities in America. There is little comment on the buildings or settings of the universities, with the book instead mostly focussing sarcastically[306] on

---

[306] Throughout *Jack Dawe and the Professors* there are various side-swipes at administrators and hierarchies and management within the university sector that are humorous for the adults reading this book rather than childhood audience.

the male academics within each setting and their weird academic lifestyle (there is a lot of going to the dining room, see Figure 4).

'The Professors' throughout are clueless academics with insular, limited views, in colonialist tales:

> Professor Stickeybeak . . . had been sent out [to Borneo] by the Oxbridge University Professors to find out all about the Takeover Tribe which they had heard was very happy, and this was a mystery because the Oxford Professors could not understand how anybody could be happy without culture and they thought that anyone who sold shrunken heads could not have any culture (ibid., p. 77).

The academics themselves are the focus, even though there are different university settings, presented without description or illustration, throughout.

'Coffee and nuts turned out to be even more successful than potatoes and sprouts and Great Uncle Barnabas became richer and richer as each year went by, and in fact he became so rich that he had to have a man, called an accountant, who spent all day counting his money for him. But he was never really happy and was always thinking how nice it would have been if he had been a Professor. One day he had an exciting thought. He realised there was no University in that part of Brazil where he farmed and so he went to the Governor of State and said that he would build and pay for a new University, to be called the Amazon University, if he could be its top Professor. The governor readily agreed provided he, the Governor himself was allowed to be the President of the University, which was also agreed. So Great Uncle Barnabas realised his life's ambition and became a top Professor and had a beautiful robe made of green and gold silk. It reached down to the ground like a lady's best party frock: in fact, before he got used to it, Uncle Barnabas tripped up and fell on his face several times.' Ibid., p. 29.

The Party

Figure 4 The Oxford Professors, with super scientist Professor Jack Dawe, and the children who accompany him on adventures. In Uncle B and Green, *Jack Dawe Super Scientist and the Professors* (p. 61), illustrated by Brian Green. Every effort has been made to trace the current right-holders, Allday Limited, Uncle B and Brian Green, who own the rights to this work: any further information is most welcome in order to remedy permissions in future editions.

The exception to this is *Mahalia Mouse Goes to College*,[307] where we see a fully illustrated university setting with detailed depictions of Harvard's redbrick campus, including pictures in the background of the diverse student population, based on a poem that was delivered as part of the award-winning actor John Lithgow's commencement speech there in 2005.[308] Mahalia is shown partaking in all aspects of campus life (even if she is a mouse in a world of humans, accepted because of her genius), appearing in lectures, theatre productions, the dormitory, cafeteria, glee club and the graduation ceremony. The lecture halls and porticos of Harvard loom behind her mouse-eye-view in a redemptive story of the transformative power of education as a means to lift oneself out of poverty, ending on commencement day (Figure 5).

Lithgow describes that his intention in writing Mahalia mouse was 'to get small children already interested in the idea of education in general and college in particular, giving them this very, very, far away goal to aim for'.[309] These three texts were all written by those with a close relationship with the university: Lewis Carroll and the mysterious 'Uncle B' being Oxford academics, Lithgow being a graduate of Harvard himself, speaking this poem

---

[307] J. Lithgow and O. Oleynikov, *Mahalia Mouse Goes to College* (New York, NY: Simon and Schuster, 2007).

[308] A new paperback edition of this text was published in July 2017, presumably to coincide with Malia Obama's acceptance to, and starting date at, Harvard University: A. Yuhas, 'Malia Obama to attend Harvard in 2017 after gap year', *The Guardian* (1 May 2016), www.theguardian.com/us-news/2016/may/01/malia-obama-attend-harvard-university-2017-gap-year.

[309] J. Lithgow, 'Actor John Lithgow Discusses Mahalia Mouse Goes to College', (2009), Simon and Schuster Books YouTube Channel, www.youtube.com/watch?v=Uwm9AUKmSu8, 4:28.

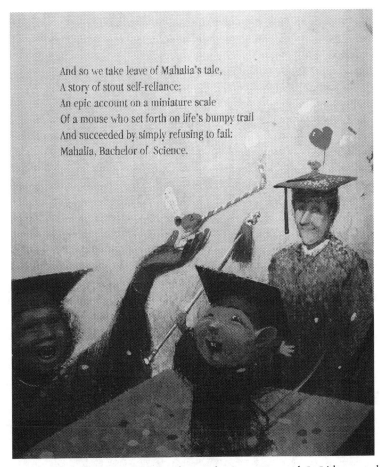

And so we take leave of Mahalia's tale,
A story of stout self-reliance;
An epic account on a miniature scale
Of a mouse who set forth on life's bumpy trail
And succeeded by simply refusing to fail:
Mahalia, Bachelor of Science.

Figure 5 Mahalia mouse celebrates her graduation at Harvard. In Lithgow and Oleynikov, *Mahalia Mouse Goes to College* (p. 39). All rights reserved, Simon and Schuster. Used with permission.

aloud at graduation there.[310] Both the satirical and inspirational take depend on insider knowledge of the university setting, and trade upon in-crowd jokes.

It is not until books created for an older childhood audience – such as *Professor Pin*,[311] the first two and last chapters of *Carney's House Party*,[312] the *His Dark Materials* trilogy,[313] *The Seven Professors of the Far North*[314] and *The Oath of the Five Lords*[315] (and, of course, Hogwarts in the *Harry Potter* series[316] if you are willing to believe the apex of the formal wizarding instructional system counts as an Higher Education institution) – that the university and its buildings routinely function as a character itself, and these are mostly textually described rather than illustrated. Our seats of learning would seem to require explanation rather than depiction.

There are three specific places on campus that appear in the background of illustrations: in a very few recent books there are lecture halls, generally showing professors professing on stage in front of a half-empty or disinterested audience (Figure 6).[317] More prevalently, in a fifth of the books there are

---

[310] Simon and Schuster, Digital Catalog, 'Mahalia Mouse Goes to College, Book and CD', (n. d.), www.simonandschuster.com/books/Mahalia-Mouse-Goes-to-College/John-Lithgow/9781416927150.

[311] Lee, *Professor Pin*.

[312] M. H. Lovelace, *Carney's House Party* (New York, NY: Harper Collings Pub, 1949).

[313] Pullman, *Northern Lights* onwards.

[314] J. Fardell, *The 7 Professors of the Far North* (London: Faber and Faber, 2004).

[315] Y. Sente and A. Juillard, *The Oath of the Five Lords* ([S. I.]: Cinebook, 2014).

[316] Rowling, *Harry Potter and the Philosopher's Stone* onwards.

[317] D. Orme and P. Richardson, *Boffin Boy and the Wizard of Edo* (Winchester: Ransom Publishing, 2006), p. 1; A. Robb, *Professor Bumblebrain's Bonkers Book on . . . God* (Farnham: CWR, 2010), p. 47; D. Noonan, *Professor Dinglebat and the Dynamic Dog De-Barker* (South Yarra: Macmillan Education Australia Publishing Pty Ltd, 2011), p. 9; see also Section 4.2.

Figure 6 Professor Mudweed lecturing, in Orme and Richardson, *Boffin Boy and the Wizard of Edo* (p. 1). Used by kind permission of David Orme and Peter Richardson.

scientific laboratories. Most of the factual books explain science, and these tend to have settings in laboratories, such as *Professor Crackinbottle and Professor Tidymind and their Two Young Helpers*,[318] *Professor I.Q. Explores the Senses*,[319] *Professor Astro Cat's Frontiers of Space*[320] and *Professor Whiskerton Presents Steampunk ABC*,[321] which explains the alphabet through clockwork Victoriana, engines, machinery and derring-do explorer's maps and zeppelins.

The scientific kit on show represents complex yet stereotypical depictions of science (there are lots of test tubes regardless of subject area). The few labs which appear in fiction are usually messy, dangerous and crammed with mysteriously complex scientific equipment.[322] The laboratory in *Professor Puffendorf's Secret Potions*,[323] which is filled with complex glassware, smoking

---

[318] Australian Government Publishing Service, Department of Education and Migrant Education Program (Australia), *Professor Crackinbottle and Professor Tidymind and Their Two Young Helpers, Barnabus and Marella: A Comic for Young Scientists* (Canberra: Australian Government Publishing Service, 1978).

[319] S. Simon and D. Kendrick, *Professor I. Q. Explores the Senses* (Honesdale, PA: Bell Books/Boyds Mills Press, 1993).

[320] D. Walliman and B. Newman, *Professor Astro Cat's Frontiers of Space* (London: Flying Eye Books, 2013), which also has scientific diagrams of the solar system, space ships, etc.

[321] L. Falkenstern, *Professor Whiskerton Presents Steampunk ABC* (Las Vegas, NV: Two Lions, 2014).

[322] A long-form poem, P. Cox, 'The Brownies in the Academy', in P. Cox (ed.), *Another Brownie Book* (New York, NY: Century Company and De Vinne Press, 1890), pp. 7–11, tells of Brownies rampaging at night-time through an Academy which 'founded by a generous hand, spread light and learning throughout the land' (ibid., p. 7), particularly playing with the scientific equipment including microscopes, crucibles and phrenology heads.

[323] R. Tzannes and K. Paul, *Professor Puffendorf's Secret Potions* (Oxford: Oxford University Press, 1992).

Figure 7 The Professor's Lecture, in Carroll, *Sylvie and Bruno Concluded* (p. 345), illustrated by Harry Furniss. Public Domain. Image from copy held at University of California Libraries, available at archive.org. Note the scientific kit he demonstrates, in an early example of a professor being aligned to a laboratory.

machinery, bicycle chains, spills, books, skulls, notebooks, furnaces, cobwebs, top-secret cabinets and gadgets including a 'Titanium Blender' and Puffendorf's own inventions, the Banana-matic and Smell-o-Telephone. Likewise, the short reader *Professor Rumbold and the Great Recycling*

Machine[324] (see Figure 12) is set in a complex factory or laboratory setting with conveyor belts, robots and gadgets. These laboratory settings require scrutiny by the reader to comprehend – or to be in awe of – the rich scientific environment: invention and science would seem to come from a place of chaos and other-worldliness.

A final place which is either mentioned within the text or referred to in illustrations is the library. Professor Inkling in *The Octonauts and the Frown Fish*[325] exclaims 'to a confused crew' when explaining what always cheers him up: 'There's nothing like perusing the printed word to stimulate the intellect and galvanize the imagination! ... To the library, my delightful colleagues!'[326]

In other texts, libraries are alluded to, or characters pass through them or book-lined studies in illustrations, without much comment or fanfare, as books are presumed to be part of the intellectual landscape. See, for example, background detail in illustrations of *Professor Johnny*,[327] The Professor in *Mistress Masham's Repose*,[328] The Administrator in *Professor Diggins Dragons*,[329] Professor Barnabus Quill and Professor Quibble in *The Rise and Fall of Mount Majestic*,[330] Professor Mortimer in *The Oath of the Five Lords*[331] and Professor

---

[324] M. Crispin, *Professor Rumbold and the Great Recycling Machine* (Leckhampton, Cheltenham: S. Thornes, 1991).

[325] Meomi, *The Octonauts and the Frown Fish* (San Francisco, CA: Immedium, 2006).

[326] Ibid., p. 23. Used with kind permission of Meomi and Immedium.

[327] Thomas, Crowell Company and Rand, Avery & Co., *Professor Johnny*.

[328] T. H. White, *Mistress Masham's Repose* (New York, NY: G. P. Putnam's Sons, 1946).

[329] F. Holman, I. Ohlsson, N. Valen and N. E. Valen, *Professor Diggins' Dragons* (New York, NY: Macmillan, 1966).

[330] J. Trafton and B. Helquist, *The Rise and Fall of Mount Majestic* (New York, NY: Puffin Books, 2010).

[331] Sente and Juillard, *The Oath of the Five Lords*.

Tobin in *Maisie Hitchins: The Case of the Feathered Mask*.[332] In addition, many of the illustrated characters hold or carry books (see Figures 8, 10, 11, 22, 23, 27and 29 in this Element), showing how important the spread of information is to their livelihoods. Books seem to be the one pictorial way that education and intellectual achievement is communicated to the childhood audience.[333]

However, laboratories, lecture halls and libraries are far from the most common of settings within the illustrations. There is a trope of academics being away from their institutional homes in order to carry out fieldwork, such as the zoologists in *Professor Twill's Travels*,[334] *Professor Wormbog in Search for the Zipperump-a-Zoo*[335] and *Professor Potts meets the Animals in Africa*;[336] the archaeologists in *The Amazing Time Travelling Adventures of Professor McGinty in Ancient Greece*[337] and *Professor Nutter and the Curse of the Pharaoh's Tomb*;[338] the palaeontologist in the *Dog that Dug*[339] and *The Case of the Crested*

[332] H. Webb, *Maisie Hitchins: The Case of the Feathered Mask* (London: Stripes, 2014).

[333] As we shall see in Figure 17, this is inverted with Professor Jim Crow's little book of wisdom, which amplifies his stupidity: D. Cory, *Little Jack Rabbit and The Squirrel Brothers* (New York, NY: Grosset and Dunlap, 1921).

[334] R. Gumpertz, *Professor Twill's Travels* (London: Ward Lock, 1968).

[335] M. Mayer, *Professor Wormbog in Search for the Zipperump-a-Zoo* (Columbus, OH: McGraw Hill Children's Publishing, 1976).

[336] K. Wright and G. Chapman, *Professor Potts Meets the Animals in Africa* (London: Watts, 1981).

[337] E. R. Reilly and R. Allen, *The Amazing Time Travelling Adventures of Professor McGinty in Ancient Greece* (Birmingham: Santiago Press, 2006).

[338] D. Webb, *Professor Nutter and the Curse of the Pharaoh's Tomb* (Blackburn: EPRINT Publishing, 2008).

[339] J. Long and K. Paul, *The Dog that Dug* (London: Bodley Head Children's Books, 1992). This was republished as J. Long and K. Paul, *The Dog Who Could Dig* (Oxford: Oxford University Press, 2008), presumably to differentiate it from S.-R. Redmond and S. Sullivan, *The Dog that Dug for Dinosaurs: A True Story* (New York, NY: Aladdin Paperbacks, 2004). Both are about dogs that unearth dinosaur bones, the 2004 book being about Mary Anning's pet dog, Tray.

Figure 8 Professor Inkling reading aloud to his more junior crew, much in the same way as reading sessions happen in pre-school settings. From Meomi, *The Octonauts and the Frown Fish* (p. 24), used with kind permission from Meomi and Immedium.

Cryptoclidus. *Professor Barrister's Dinosaur Mysteries*,[340] and Professor Mackenzie, the explorer in the *Maisie* series.[341] Most of the action in *Professor Puffendorf's Secret Potions*[342] happens in her lab when she is away at a conference, and *Dr Dog* travels away to a conference[343] and then on holiday.[344] Academics are rarely at their university: as a result, it is a place seldom presented to the readers of these children's books, either in illustration or description. Paradoxically, universities are not explained to children through books, perhaps as they are thought not to be known to them: but universities are not known to children as they are not explained as part of the media produced for a child audience.

Academics are not depicted as being part of institutions: they mostly work alone. Twenty-two of the 289 books feature pairs or triples of professors working together – or against each other – in the same text (for example, Professor Gylden Lox and Dr Med Yusa run a hairdressing academy[345]). The largest number of individually named academics in a single book is four, working together in a lab in *Mad Professor: Concoct Extremely Weird Science Projects*.[346] Two books briefly feature exclusively male scholarly societies and

---

[340] S. Penner, *The Case of the Crested Cryptoclidus. Professor Barrister's Dinosaur Mysteries* (Seattle, WA: Ring of Fire Publishing, 2012).

[341] A. Paterson, *Maisie Comes to Morningside* (Galashiels: Byway Books, 1984), onwards. Mackenzie is not described as an academic until later books in the series: he is Doctor Mackenzie in A. Paterson, *Maisie in the Rainforest* (Broxburn: Glowworm Book Ltd., 1992, p. 26) and Professor Mackenzie in A. Paterson, *Maisie Digs Up the Past* (Broxburn: Glowworm Book Ltd., 1994, p. 7).

[342] Tzannes and Paul, *Professor Puffendorf's Secret Potions.* [343] Cole, *Dr Dog.*

[344] Cole, *A Dose of Dr Dog.*

[345] A. Brownfeather and Wright Group, Incorporated, *Professor Gylden Lox's Hair School* (Bothell, WA: Wright Group, 2002).

[346] M. Frauenfelder, *Mad Professor: Concoct Extremely Weird Science Projects – Robot Food, Saucer Slime, Martian Volcanoes and More* (Vancouver: Raincoast Books and San Francisco, CA: Chronicle Books LLC, 2002).

all-male academic panels: the scientific committee in *Moon Man*[347] and the 'Wise Professors of Prague' in *The Wicked Tricks of Till Owlyglass*.[348] *Jack Dawe Super Scientist and the Professors* has its packs of dons.[349] However, in the majority of the corpus, in 267 books, the academics are lone figures acting independently, generally away from the institution: academia is mostly portrayed as a singular, even lonely, endeavour, which mimics the upholding of the myth of the lone scholar emanating from the academy itself: see Grendler's analysis of depictions of lone scholars in the Italian Renaissance[350] and Algazi's analysis of depictions of studies in Early Modern European Cultures.[351] This is in stark contrast to family stories that dominate children's literature.[352] 'Like small children who play on their own, main characters in preschool literature act alone … they make their decisions based on their need to discover how the world works for them':[353] lone academics are set up as adult counterparts to the lone child reader, experiencing difference together.

More than half of these academics are depicted in their household environment rather than in a university setting. The distinction between work and home is blurred by the fact that many carry out scientific experiments on

---

[347] T. Ungerer, *Moon Man* (New York, NY: Phaidon Press, 1966). Featured on Congrats, you have an all male panel!, 'All male panels also in kids books!' (23 May 2015) http://allmalepanels.tumblr.com/post/119647170216/all-male-panels-also-in-kids-books on Tumblr.

[348] M. Rosen, *The Wicked Tricks of Till Owlyglass* (London: Walker Books, 1990).

[349] Uncle B and Green, *Jack Dawe Super Scientist and the Professors*.

[350] P. F. Grendler, *The Universities of the Italian Renaissance* (JHU Press, 2002).

[351] G. Algazi, 'At the Study: Notes on the Production of the Scholarly Self', *Space and Self in Early Modern European Cultures* (University of Toronto Press, 2012), pp. 17–50.

[352] Grenby, *Children's Literature*, p. 117.

[353] J. P. May, *Children's Literature and Critical Theory: Reading and Writing for Understanding* (Oxford: Oxford University Press, 1994), p. 40.

their own property, which are therefore not the type of homes that the book's readership would typically live in. For example, Professor Mickimecki has a barn workshop with a windmill on the roof, scientifically kitted out, and big enough to build submarines in.[354] Professor Nut 'lived in an old house in the oldest part of town',[355] and it is there that he has a laboratory where he can record an avant garde (tuneless!) symphony with his friend Professor Crotchet. Professor Oliver Query has a spaceship in his yard, 'a telescope on the roof, and a weather-vane that pointed in two directions at once. There was even an anchored flying saucer'.[356] This focus on the home of the person as the locus for the intellect stresses the importance of the academic individual rather than the higher education institution within the children's literature genre. It is interactions within these homes that situate the plot: the starting setting of *The Lion, The Witch and the Wardrobe* is Professor Digory Kirke's isolated house, 'in the heart of the country, ten miles from the nearest railway station and two miles from the nearest post-office' which was 'so old and famous that people from all over England used to come and ask permission to see over it'.[357] *Cockatoos*[358] centres around the birds of a baffled professor, which decide to hide all over his large house. *The Mysterious Collection of*

---

[354] J. Wahl, *SOS Bobmobile* (Harmondsworth: Puffin Books, 1977).

[355] A. Blackwood and C. Skilton, *Doctor Crotchet's Symphony* (London: Evans Brothers Limited, 1977), p. 5. Used by kind permission of Alan Blackwood.

[356] S. Odgers and C. Nye, *My Father the Mad Professor* (Auckland: Shortland Publications, 1997), p. 19. Used by kind permission of Sally Odgers.

[357] Lewis, *The Lion, the Witch and the Wardrobe*, p. 1 and p. 51. THE LION, THE WITCH AND THE WARDROBE by C. S. Lewis © copyright CS Lewis Pte Ltd 1950. Used by kind permission.

[358] Q. Blake, *Cockatoos* (London: Red Fox, 1992).

Dr David Harleyson[359] features a treasure hunt around his mansion, with no indication of why he would be called Dr in the first place, given he is a 'famous artist'[360] – with the treasure hunt ending in the most domestic of rituals: Dr Harleyson's marriage. The individual, and the individual's home, is the focus here, but homes are different to usual suburban living, often being large, messy mansions full of antiquities, oil paintings and silverware. Professor Digory Kirke's House is full of 'the pictures and the armour, and the rare books in the library'.[361] These strange abodes give some sense of the other-worldliness of the academics:

> At that moment, the passageway opened out into a large room. Sunlight filtered through the narrow windows, showing the strange hieroglyphics covering the walls. Broken jars, some with lids with animal heads covered the tables, and bits of old stone littered the floor. There was dust everywhere. Dust and pawprints.
>
> 'It's not like a proper house,' I said. 'There's hardly any furniture. Just a lot of . . . rubbish.'
>
> 'Ancient objects, you mean,' said a familiar voice, and Dr Sphinx appeared from a hidden door in the far wall. [Pictured wearing a safari suit and pith helmet see Figure 9][362].

---

[359] J. Cassels, *The Mysterious Collection of Dr David Harleyson* (New York, NY: Walker & Co., 2004).

[360] Ibid., p. 1. [361] Lewis, *The Lion, the Witch and the Wardrobe*, p. 51.

[362] M. Ryan, *Weird Street: The Riddle of Dr Sphinx* (London: A&C Black, 2009), pp. 36–7. © Margaret Ryan, 1997, Weird Street: The Riddle of Dr Sphinx and A&C Black Children's and Educational, an imprint of Bloomsbury Publishing Plc. Quoted by kind permission.

Figure 9 Dr Sphinx's living room. In Ryan, *Weird Street: The Riddle of Dr Sphinx*, © Margaret Ryan, 1997, Weird Street: The Riddle of Dr Sphinx and A&C Black Children's and Educational, an imprint of Bloomsbury Publishing Plc, p. 37. Used with permission. Not your normal interior household design.

It is therefore not universities or higher education *per se* that are of interest in texts marketed towards a childhood audience, but the people who belong to the university – the professors and doctors – and their lifestyle and characteristics, that are presented to readers. By meeting them in their

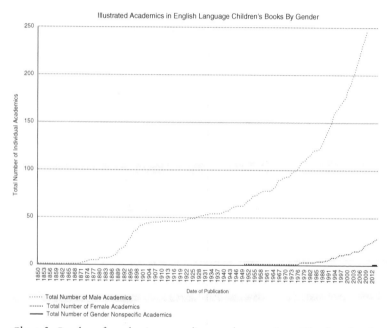

Chart 3 Gender of academics, revealing totals over time. The first female student appears in 1949, and the first female academic did not appear until 1950. Although there has been a growth in the total number of books featuring academics, they are still mostly men. Non-gender-specific individuals are not an important factor in the corpus.

home environment, we can see the differences in how they choose to live, and what a 'life of the mind' involves, in a location where children can come into contact with them easily. These individuals, in turn, come to represent the university, and intellectual achievement, in children's literature. As a result, this analysis will focus on the representations of academics across the corpus, the stereotypes that emerge, and the influences and perceptions that endure.

4.4 Gender

The most striking element of the corpus is gender: of 328 academics, 298 are men and twenty-nine are women (9 per cent), with only one having an ambiguous gender identity (Chart 3). The delineation between heterosexual gender norms is pronounced, and even with the five unseen narrators, or animal or inanimate object academics, it is easy to determine gender, given names, pronouns and physical characteristics. This difference between male and female characters accrues over time, and this visualisation demonstrates the dominance of male characters.

This discrepancy between male and female academics can be explained in two ways. Firstly, it has to be acknowledged that, despite the admission of women to study in many places of higher education in English-speaking areas from the late nineteenth century, women were mostly barred from taking up academic positions until the late twentieth century.[363] There is still a range of 'structural-institutional, social, and cultural factors' that explain women's current woeful underrepresentation in academic life.[364] Across Europe in 2015, only 20 per cent of full professors were female.[365] There were therefore, and are therefore, few women in society who have a senior academic role and the corpus

---

[363] B. M. Solomon, *In the Company of Educated Women: A History of Women and Higher Education in America* (Yale University Press, 1985); A. M. M. Alemán and K. A. Renn, *Women in Higher Education: An Encyclopedia* (ABC-CLIO, 2002); L. S. Hornig, *Equal Rites, Unequal Outcomes: Women in American Research Universities* (Springer Science & Business Media, 2003).

[364] C. Luke, *Globalization and Women in Academia: North/West–South/East* (Routledge, 2001), p. vii.

[365] European Commission, 'She Figures 2015'. Research and Innovation Report, Science With And For Society Programme (2015), https://ec.europa.eu/

reflects this expected discrepancy in the profession. Secondly, the corpus is only of *fictional* academics, and it would have been reasonable to hope that authors' imaginations could reflect possibilities and depict contemporary impossibilities or aspirations rather than to entrench realities: unfortunately, children's literature seems to veer towards safe, established, dominant tropes that allow plots to develop without much explanation, rather than behaving imaginatively.[366] This, however, has the effect of reiterating and reinforcing social inequalities. The incentives and discincentives for the publishing of 'radical' children's literature that exposes unjust power structures and promotes social justice are covered in Mickenberg and Nel,[367] although, as we shall see in Section 6, the current digital environment seems to be finally marrying publishers with an audience for such material.[368]

research/swafs/pdf/pub_gender_equality/she_figures_2015-final.pdf#view=fit&pagemode=none, p. 127.

[366] There is little room here to explore the thorny issue of what children's literature is *for*, or how to perceive texts which can simultaneously instruct, educate, amuse, terrify and comfort (and beyond!) a heterogeneous readership who will each respond individually to a text: see J. Rose, *The Case of Peter Pan, or The Impossibility of Children's Fiction* (Philadelphia: University of Pennsylvania Press, 1984), P. Nodelman, *The Pleasures of Children's Literature* (Longman Pub Group, 1996), L. R. Sipe, 'Children's response to literature: author, text, reader, context', *Theory into Practice*, 38(3), (1999), 120–129 and J. Zipes, *Sticks and Stones: The Troublesome Success of Children's Literature from Slovenly Peter to Harry Potter* (Routledge, 2013) for these wider issues.

[367] J. L. Mickenberg and P. Nel, 'Radical children's literature now!', *Children's Literature Association Quarterly*, 36(4), (2011), pp. 445–473; see also K. Reynolds, *Radical Children's Literature: Future Visions and Aesthetic Transformations in Juvenile Fiction* (Springer, 2007). and J. L. Mickenberg and P. Nel, (eds.), *Tales for Little Rebels: A Collection of Radical Children's Literature* (NYU Press, 2008).

[368] E. Favilli and F. Cavallo, *Good Night Stories for Rebel Girls: 100 Tales of Extraordinary Women* (London: Timbuktu Labs, 2016).

The first female in our corpus is a student, Carney Sibley, in the early and final chapters of *Carney's House Party* published in 1949, a fictional account of the time around the summer break at the then all-female Vassar College in the United States.[369] Although Carney clearly loves the campus, the novel focuses more on her engagement and her future as a wife than on her education. Shortly after, the first female professor appears in the corpus – a full hundred years after the first male, when there are already sixty-eight males; Professor Jocelyn Mabel Peabody, who appears in the *Eagle* comic (1950 onwards) as Space Fleet's Permanent Special Advisor to the Exploration and Research Department and a regular sidekick to Dan Dare. She is a product of the imagination of the writers, with her blue-chip academic backstory[370] including a doctorate from Magdalen College, Oxford, being impossible at the time of writing.[371] Set in the mid to late 1980s, the writers saw the future of science as

[369] Founded in 1861, Vassar becoming co-educational in 1969 – see Vassar College, 'A History of Vassar College', Vassar info (n. d.), https://info.vassar.edu/about/ vassar/history.html – and Carney's story documents the experience of a female student within many of the women-only academies in the United States at the time. Carney sings a few lines of the *Young Matthew Vassar* college song in the text, which lauds the founder and shows her emotional attachment to the university: 'It occurred to him, injustice had been done to women's brains/What a pity undeveloped they should be . . . So Matthew, Mathew Vassar/Built a college then and there for me and you . . .' (A.L. Reed 'Young Matthew Vassar' 1892, in Vassar College, *Alumnae Anniversary Song-Book* (New York, NY: Vassar College Associate Alumnae/G. Schirmer, June 1921), https://digitallibrary.vassar.edu/islandora/object/vassar% 3A21635#page/1/mode/1up, p. 12, part quoted in Lovelace, *Carney's House Party*, p. 3).

[370] Presented in full in M. Higgs and N. Wright, *The Dan Dare Dossier: Celebrating the 40th Anniversary of Dan Dare, Pilot of the Future* (London: Hawk Books, 1990), p. 16.

[371] The archivist at Magdalen College confirmed that women were accepted there from 1979, with the first female doctoral student graduating in 1982 (B. Taylor, Reply to

including women. Dan Dare's creator and artist, Frank Hampson, said of Peabody when interviewed in 1974:

> I didn't want to produce a strip without a female. In a way I struck a blow for Women's Lib! She was shown as a very clever, attractive young lady. It also paved the way for a few arguments between her and [the men] in the first story – a nice human touch ... she was just a very normal, efficient, competent girl.[372]

However, Professor Peabody encounters significant bias and approbation at every turn, see Figure 10.

Unfortunately, Professor Peabody is an outlier (and featured in a comic rather than a codex). The first illustrated female academic in a book, after sixty-nine males are already in the corpus, is a 'researcher' and mother, not even given a name as the focus in on her male employer and her son, in *Professor Coconut and the Thief* (Figure 11):

> Professor Albert is the head of our group of anthropologists. My mother is an anthropologist. We came to Africa to dig for bones of animals and people who lived millions of years ago.[373]

email from Melissa Terras, 'Question regarding first woman to teach/undertake a DPhil at Magdalen', 12 July 2016). The fictional future career of Professor Peabody almost aligns with reality, given that the action of Dan Dare begins in the mid-1980s, after Peabody has graduated.

[372] A. Vince, *The Frank Hampson Interview* (Cambridge: Astral Publications in association with the Eagle Society, 1994). Quoted in D. Jones and T. Watkins, *A Necessary Fantasy? The Heroic Figure in Children's Popular Culture* (Routledge, 2000), p. 27.

[373] R. G. Gelman and J. Richter, *Professor Coconut and the Thief*, illustrated by E. Arnold McCully (New York, NY: Holt, Rinehart and Winston, 1977), p. 12

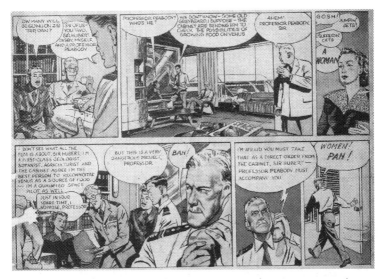

Figure 10 Professor Peabody's first appearance, as she joins Dan Dare's team in *Eagle*, 12 May 1950 (Vol. 1 No 5). She holds a book as a symbol of her professional status. Reproduced with kind permission of the Dan Dare Corporation Limited.

The Doctor of Literature in *The Pirates Mixed-Up Voyage*[374] is not given her academic title, being known as Mrs Hatchett.[375] The female palaeontologist in *The*

[374] Mahy and Chamberlain, *The Pirate's Mixed-Up Voyage*.

[375] This is echoed in the real-life academy, where women are less likely to be addressed by professional title than men, particularly when introduced by men: J. A. Files, A. P. Mayer, M. G. Ko et al., 'Speaker introductions at internal medicine grand rounds: forms of address reveal gender bias', *Journal of Women's Health* 26(5), (May 2017), 413–419, https://doi.org/10.1089/jwh.2016.6044.

Figure 11 The female anthropologist in Gelman and Richter, *Professor Coconut and the Thief* (p. 13), an outsider to the male argument led by Professor Albert, who is renamed Professor Coconut by the children. Note that she is holding paperwork, even in the jungle. Illustrated by Emily Arnold McCully, used with kind permission.

Professor Rumbold worked hard on the design.

3

Figure 12 Professor Rumbold, the first named female in the corpus. Note the robots in the background which interact with the child reader, as the professor concentrates on the technology. In Crispin, *Professor Rumbold and the Great Recycling Machine* (p. 3). Illustrated by Alan Rowe. Used with kind permission of Mavis Crispin and Alan Rowe.

Dog That Dug is not given a name.[376] The first book to contain a *named* female professor is the short scholastic reader, *Professor Rumbold and the Great Recycling Machine* (1991) (Figure 12), in which she calmly designs technology to deal with the world's growing environmental crisis, in a reader published to support the introduction of Science into the new UK National Curriculum in schools.[377]

There are significantly fewer females than should be expected given the current statistics of real-life academia: even over the five-year period 2009–14 there are fifty-nine male academics to only seven females (12 per cent) in the corpus, which is half of the number that would be expected in the real-life academy in this recent period. We are reminded that males routinely out-number females as protagonists in children's literature,[378] that 'female char-acters . . . in award-winning pictures books [are] almost non-existent and, when present, [are] stereotypically passive and domestic'.[379] 'Male characters are twice as likely to take leading roles in children's picture books and are given far more speaking parts than females.'[380] A quarter of children's books have no female characters at all, and this 'symbolic annihilation' has 'implications for

---

[376] Long and Paul, *The Dog that Dug*.

[377] M. Crispin, Personal communication: 'Professor Rumbold and the Great Recycling Machine', reply to email from Melissa Terras, 3 April 2017.

[378] E. Grauerholz and B. A. Pescosolido, 'Gender representation in children's literature: 1900–1984', *Gender & Society*, 3(1), (1989), 113–125; A. M. Gooden and M. A. Gooden, 'Gender representation in notable children's picture books: 1995–1999', *Sex Roles*, 45(1–2), (2001), pp. 89–101; D. Ferguson, 'Must monsters always be male? Huge gender bias revealed in children's books', *The Observer* (Sunday, 21 January 2018), www.theguardian.com/books/2018/jan/21/childrens-books-sex ism-monster-in-your-kids-book-is-male.

[379] Clark, 'Why all the counting? Feminist social science research on children's literature', p. 286.

[380] Ferguson, 'Must monsters always be male?'

children's understandings of gender'.[381] Will this proportion of professors in children's books change as time goes on, with the growing public perception of women being part of the academy? Or does this erasure contribute to children's perception of appropriate gender roles, and so reinforce inequalities?

The female academics are illustrated in books published in the United Kingdom (18), the United States (9) and Canada (2): showing how lacking the representation of intelligent, authoritative females are in the rest of the English speaking world's children's literature (7 % of the total corpus comes from three countries: Australia, 5 %, India, 2 % and New Zealand, 1 %; there is not a female academic to be found among these, nor in the single books published in Ireland, Germany, South Africa and Singapore). Women are so lacking as protagonists that the surprise denouement of a 'choose your own adventure' book hinges upon the fact that a missing professor is actually female, and you didn't expect that, did you? (*Whatever Happened To Professor Potts?: Follow the Clues to Unravel the Mystery.*[382] Apologies for the spoiler.) In addition, the illustrations featured in the American editions of the Harry Potter novels[383] concentrate on the male academics: Dumbledore, Snape and Quirrell;[384] Lockhart;[385] Mad-Eyed Moody and Hagrid;[386] Firenze and Lupin;[387] Slughorn.[388] The only two

---

[381] J. McCabe, E. Fairchild, L. Grauerholz, B. A. Pescosolido and D. Tope, 'Gender in twentieth-century children's books: patterns of disparity in titles and central characters', *Gender & Society*, 25(2), (2011), 197–226, p. 197.

[382] P. Roxbee Cox and S. Atkinson, *Whatever Happened to Professor Potts? Follow the Clues to Unravel the Mystery* (London: Usborne, 1995).

[383] Rowling, *Harry Potter and the Sorcerer's Stone* onwards.

[384] Rowling, *Harry Potter and the Sorcerer's Stone*.

[385] Rowling, *Harry Potter and the Chamber of Secrets*.

[386] Rowling, *Harry Potter and the Goblet of Fire*.

[387] Rowling, *Harry Potter and the Order of the Phoenix*.

[388] Rowling, *Harry Potter and the Half-Blood Prince*.

Elements in Publishing and Book Culture

Now it's raining heavily. Professor Boffin has opened his umbrella and Mrs Boffin is looking at it. "This umbrella's full of holes," she says. "You need a new umbrella, dear. You must buy a new umbrella!"

Now they are home. Their clothes are very wet. "Look at my hair," Mrs Boffin says. "It's very wet. And look at my clothes! They're full of water!" But the Professor isn't listening. He's thinking.

Figure 13 How can professors keep dry without a wife to help them? In Alexander, *Professor Boffin's Umbrella* (p. 3). Every effort has been made to trace the current right-holders of this work (L. G. Alexander and Longman publishers): any further information is most welcome in order to remedy permissions in future editions.

female professors illustrated are Trelawney[389] and Umbridge:[390] Professor Minerva McGonagall, although a central maternal figure within all the Harry Potter books, is omitted from any illustration in any English language edition published prior to 2015.

There *are* plenty of women in the 289 books, but they tend to be wives and housekeepers who very visibly provide stability and practical support for the helplessly dependent academics, such as the wife in the 'Structural Reader', *Professor Boffin's Umbrella* (Figure 13).[391]

Or:

> Miss Lavender sighed heavily. After thirty years, she was used to the Professor's absent-minded ways, but she did believe in sitting down to tea when it was served ...[392]
>
> 'Just a minute,' said Miss Lavender. 'I've left the oven on.'
>
> The Professor muttered something old-fashioned about women and science, but he waited patiently till she returned (Figure 14).[393]

Or:

> [T]here they were, in a big cloud of smoke and dust, back in the Professor's garden. Mrs Smith was on her back doorstep, hands on

---

[389] Rowling, *Harry Potter and the Chamber of Secrets*; Rowling, *Harry Potter and the Prisoner of Azkaban*.

[390] Rowling, *Harry Potter and the Order of the Phoenix*.

[391] L. G. Alexander, *Professor Boffin's Umbrella* (London: Longman, 1970).

[392] A. Englander, *The Amazing Professor and his Travels in Time* (London: Methuen Children's, 1983), p. 4.

[393] Ibid., p. 6. Used by kind permission of Egmont Publishing.

Figure 14 Professor Magnus MacWhizzer is fawned upon by his long-suffering housekeeper in Englander, *The Amazing Professor and his Travels in Time* (p. 26). The children pictured are his great-great-niece and nephew, relieved they have returned safely after time-travel did not go to plan. Used with kind permission of Egmont Publishing.

Figure 15 Professor P. Brain's disdain for household chores. In McLeay, *Professor P. Brain's Astronomical Trip* (p. 32). Illustrated by "Mark Fenton and his computer", in the first obviously digital illustration. Every effort has been made to trace the current right-holders, Arnold-Wheaton Publishers, Anna McLeay and Mark Fenton, who own the rights to this work: any further information is most welcome in order to remedy permissions in future editions.

hips, very angry indeed. Her washing was covered in soot and coal dust. But there was no time for the Professor ... to apologise (Figure 15).[394]

And (indicating that this trope is not outdated, but enduring):

Mrs Molecule had given [Professor Molecule] his own key once, but she had had to replace it more than six times before kindly suggesting that maybe he should just knock when he came home and therefore not to worry about such trivial things as door keys.[395]

Professor Digory Kirke has a housekeeper called Mrs Macready and three female servants.[396] Professor Euclid Bullfinch has a housekeeper, Mrs Dunn, whose son Danny accompanies the Professor on adventures.[397] Professor Diggins relies heavily on his wife for dressing and feeding.[398] Dr Xargle relies on Matron to undertake practical elements of student activities.[399] Professor Dupont has a cook called Hortense.[400] Professor Mortimer has a housekeeper called Mrs Benson.[401] Over and over, women are shown in subservient positions, in little change from what Nilsen noted as long ago as 1971 that the

---

[394] A. McLeay, *Professor P. Brain's Astronomical Trip* (Leeds: Arnold Wheaton, 1987), p. 31.

[395] A. Wyatt, *Professor Molecule's Fantastic Listening Machine* (Gobie Publishing, 2006).

[396] Lewis *The Lion, the Witch and the Wardrobe*, p. 1.

[397] Williams and Abrashkin, *Danny Dunn and the Anti-Gravity Paint*.

[398] Holman, Ohlsson, Valen and Valen, *Professor Diggins' Dragons*.

[399] Willis and Ross, *Dr Xargle's Book of Earthlets* onwards [400] Blake, *Cockatoos*.

[401] Sente and Juillard, *The Oath of the Five Lords*.

majority of women in children's books are 'token females ... [who] stand in doorways ... look through windows ... unobtrusive'.[402] There are parallels here with campus novels written for adults about the university system: in an analysis of which Showalter noted, 'I was always hoping to find stories of women professors ... I've been sharply aware of the women who appear in the background, as students, as eccentric dons and dames, and especially as faculty wives'.[403]

The women academics do not have partners or assistants, with the exception of Professor Puffendorf, who has a male lab assistant – Enzo – but the story revolves around his jealousy, and what happens when he chooses to disobey Puffendorf's instructions when she is away.[404] The men may have wives and housekeepers to assist them but there is an absence of their own offspring. Only one woman and seven men are noted as being parents: the unnamed female anthropologist in *Professor Coconut and the Thief* mentioned by her son, the childhood narrator (no father is in the text);[405] the mostly absent scientific father in *The Professor's Children*,[406] Professor Hayling, loving father of Tinker and a friend of Uncle Quentin[407] in *Five Are Together Again*,[408] the mysterious Professor Gamma, who involves his daughter

[402] Nilsen, 'Women in Children's Literature', p. 919.

[403] Showalter, *Faculty Towers: The Academic Novel and its Discontents*, p. 16.

[404] Tzannes and Paul, *Professor Puffendorf's Secret Potions*.

[405] Gelman and Richter, *Professor Coconut and the Thief*.

[406] E. H. Fowler and E. K. Burgess, *The Professor's Children* (London: Longman's, Green, 1898).

[407] It is likely that George's father in *The Famous Five*, Quentin Kirrin, is also a University professor, as he is described as a famous scientist and inventor, and a colleague of Professor Hayling, but he is never given an affiliation or title.

[408] E. Blyton, *Five Are Together Again* (London: Hodder and Stoughton, 1963).

Kiryl in a series of science fiction adventures,[409] Professor Mackenzie, absent explorer father who leaves his daughter *Maisie* with her grandmother,[410] Lord Asriel, who has placed his daughter into the care of others,[411] and Professor Oliver Query, who is reunited with his daughter after she had been living with her mother, in *My Father the Mad Professor*, although 'I have no ambition to be a normal father'.[412] The father in 'The Mad Professor's Daughter' is never seen, but his fearful presence, while out of sight, is terrifying.[413] The gender of the parent is usually juxtaposed with the opposite gender of child, with the majority being (absent) male professors with daughters. There are three uncles: Dr Ivor Dare, Dan Dare's uncle;[414] Professor Dinglebat, 'we're so lucky to have an uncle who's a famous professor';[415] and The Evil Professor in *Tetrax the Swamp Crocodile* in the Sea Quest series;[416] and one Great-Great-Grand-Uncle, Professor Magnus MacWhizzer in *The Amazing Professor and His Travels in Time*.[417] However, there are no academic aunts. Although many academics are depicted in the place where family stories are usually set – the home – the academics are normally not in a family environment (nor a

---

[409] F. Hoyle and G. Hoyle, *The Frozen Planet of Azuron* (London: Ladybird, 1982) onwards.

[410] Paterson, *Maisie Comes to Morningside* onwards [411] Pullman, *Northern Lights*.

[412] Odgers and Nye, *My Father the Mad Professor*, p. 21.

[413] A. Ahlberg, 'The Mad Professor's Daughter', in A. Ahlberg, *Heard It in the Playground*, illustrated by Fritz Wegner (Viking Kestrel, 1989), pp. 67–72.

[414] Eagle, 'Dan Dare', 2(26), (London: Hulton Press, 5 October 1951).

[415] Noonan, *Professor Dinglebat and the Dynamic Dog De-Barker*, p. 7. Used by kind permission of The McGraw-Hill Companies Inc.

[416] A. Blade, *Sea Quest: Tetrax the Swamp Crocodile* (London: Orchard, 2014).

[417] Englander, *The Amazing Professor and his Travels in Time*.

typical home environment, given their houses are so strange), which sets up a different mechanism for plot and theme given that 'probably the majority of children's fiction has been set within the family'.[418] Interactions with unrelated children spur on plot lines and challenge scientific stereotypes, which will be explored in Section 4.12.

It is worth noting that, although only 9 per cent of the academics in the corpus are female, ninety-two (32 per cent) of the 289 books have an identifiably female author, and thirty-three have a female illustrator, showing the dominance of male creative influence in the corpus.[419] Of the 29 female academics, sixteen are authored, and nine illustrated, by women. Both male and female authors have preferred to write about dominant male academics and subservient females who facilitate and enable their intellectual brilliance, although female authors are more likely to include female academic characters.

It can be difficult to introduce ambiguity, or to get away from male dominance, in children's picture books: the author and illustrator of *Traction Man is Here* (2005), Mini Grey, said: 'There's an issue I often face with picture book characters – that when I want to make them gender-neutral, I make them vaguely male rather than female – but really I want them not to have a gender'.[420] Subtle characteristics can be both introduced by the author and/or perceived by the reader, to reinforce the 'implicit biases'

---

[418] Grenby, *Children's Literature*, p. 117.

[419] Using https://genderize.io as a tool to determine the gender of a first name, although this is not an exact process.

[420] M. Grey, Personal communication: 'Evil Dr Sock and Wicked Professor Spade – quick question about conventions', reply to email from Melissa Terras, 2 February 2017.

we all have regarding gender.[421] Only one character in the corpus has an deliberately playful, ambiguous gender identity: an unspecified narratorial voice which may or may not be the female child of colour on the cover of, or one of the boys inside, *Professor Cook's Mind-Blowing Bakes*.[422] Debbie Foy, the Managing Editor of Wayland, part of Hachette Children's Books, confirmed:

> 'Professor Cook' was originally intended to be 'faceless' and was probably envisaged as the stereotypical white-haired, white, male, science prof, but when we did the photo shoot and started to put the covers together we really liked the idea of subverting the stereotype with a black girl who could be identified (on the cover at least) as 'Professor Cook'. We then counterbalanced it on the inside with boys in the professor/cooking role, as we seek to sell to a broad educational/library market and of course these kinds of issues are key.[423]

This response from a present day publisher of children's books suggests that they are both aware of the gender inequalities of children's literature

---

[421] C. L. Ridgeway and S. J. Correll, 'Unpacking the gender system: a theoretical perspective on gender beliefs and social relations', *Gender & Society*, 18(4), (2004), 510–531.

[422] Brash, *Professor Cook's Mind-Blowing Bakes*.

[423] D. Foy, Personal communication: 'Professor Cook', reply to email from Melissa Terras, 2 February 2013.

and hoping to overcome them, through creative ambiguity and playing with established stereotypes. Challenging the dominance of the male in children's literature can only happen if done deliberately and imaginatively.

4.5 Race

Fictional academics are predominantly white. There are only seven who are visibly of black, Asian or minority ethnic descent, and only three of these are actually adults within a university: a Chinese Professor, in *Rollo's Journey to Cambridge*,[424] a Professor of Linguistics in *Points of View with Professor Peekaboo*,[425] and Professor Wiseman, the science museum director, in the later instantiations of the *Curious George* book series.[426] The remainder invoke the term 'professor' to suggest intelligence: a charlatan professor in a Chinese folk tale,[427] one child so intelligent he is called 'The Prof' in *Henry's Baby*,[428] and two

[424] J. T. Wheelwright and F. J. Stimson, *Rollo's Journey to Cambridge*, illustrated by F. G. Attwood (Boston, MA: A. Williams and Co., 1880), p. 16.

[425] J. Agard and S. Kitamura, *Points of View with Professor Peekaboo: Poems* (London: Bodley Head Children's Books, 2000).

[426] M. Rey and H. A. Rey, *Curious George's Dinosaur Discovery* (Boston, MA: Houghton Mifflin, 2006) onwards.

[427] L. Yep and D. Wiesner, *The Rainbow People* (New York, NY: HarperTrophy, 1989).

[428] M. Hoffman and S. Winter, *Henry's Baby* (London and New York, NY: Dorling Kindersley, 1993).

Elements in Publishing and Book Culture

Figure 16 The change of Professor Wiseman, Science Museum Director, and erstwhile Rocket Scientist, in the Curious George series. Left: 1957 original version (seated at desk). Illustration from CURIOUS GEORGE GETS A MEDAL by H. A. Rey © 1957 and renewed 1985 by Margaret E. Rey. Reprinted with permission of Houghton Mifflin Harcourt Publishing Company.[429] All rights reserved. In Rey and Rey, *The Complete Adventures of Curious George* (p. 189). Right, 2010 version. Illustration from CURIOUS GEORGE AND THE SURPRISE GIFT by H. A. Rey © 2008. Reprinted with permission of Houghton Mifflin Harcourt Publishing Company. All rights reserved.[430]

[429] In M. Rey and H. A. Rey, 'Curious George gets a medal', in M. Rey and H. A. Rey, *The Complete Adventures of Curious George* (Boston, MA: Houghton Mifflin Harcourt, 1957, 2001).

[430] In H. Rey, *Curious George Storybook Collection* (Boston, MA: Houghton Mifflin Harcourt, 2010), p. 68.

of the children in *The Preschool Professors Learn How Seeds Grow*.[431] This inclusion of visibly, culturally different races in these few examples is a recent response to the long-noted white hegemony of children's literature.[432] In fact, Professor Wiseman in the *Curious George* series changes both gender and race over the course of the franchise, turning from a stereotypical white academic male to a friendly, female 'American, likely with Indian ancestry',[433] in the latest range of books that accompany the PBS television cartoon series running since

---

[431] K. Bale, *The Preschool Professors Learn How Seeds Grow* (Mustang, OK: Tate Publishing & Enterprises, 2012). In addition, Professor Cook in Brash, *Professor Cook's Mind-Blowing Bakes* may or may not be a girl of colour, as above. There are illustrated characters of colour in the background of Lithgow and Oleynikov, *Mahalia Mouse Goes to College* (see Figure 5), who are presumably students, but these are unnamed, so are not included following the methodology, although this inclusive approach is a welcome addition to the children's literature landscape.

[432] N. Larrick, 'The all-white world of children's books', *Saturday Review*, 48(11), (1965), pp. 63–65; B. A. Pescosolido, E. Grauerholz and M. A. Milkie, 'Culture and conflict: the portrayal of Blacks in US children's picture books through the mid- and late-twentieth century', *American Sociological Review* (1997), pp. 443–464; G. Klein, *Reading into Racism: Bias in Children's Literature and Learning Materials* (Routledge, 2002); Cooperative Children's Book Center School of Education, 'Publishing Statistics on Children's Books about People of Color and First/Native Nations and by People of Color and First/Native Nations Authors and Illustrators', (2015), https://ccbc.education .wisc.edu/books/pcstats.asp#black.

[433] Curious George Wiki, 'Professor Wiseman' (n. d.), http://curious-george.wikia .com/wiki/Professor_Wiseman.

" Here's Your Little Book."
Little Jack Rabbit and Professor Crow.   *Frontispiece—(Page 43)*

Figure 17 Professor Jim Crow in *Cory, Little Jack Rabbit and Professor Crow*
(Frontispiece). Public Domain, author's own copy.

2006: this indicates how issues of diversity can be influenced by external pressures (Figure 16).[434]

There are also not-so-subtle racist undertones to be found. The Chinese Professor in *Rollo's Journey to Cambridge* is described as a 'yellow-skinned gentleman with eyes cut bias'[435] and is not allowed to be more than an oriental caricature. Professor Jim Crow, a forgetful but kindly blackbird, who knows little about how the world operates without double-checking it first in his book of wisdom that doesn't seem to explain anything, appears in the *Little Jack Rabbit* series,[436] particularly in *Little Jack Rabbit and Professor Crow* (Figure 17).[437] These stories for children were first

---

[434] This was probably at the behest of the television production company, which then affected the illustrated books accompanying the series. Curious George has been accused on insensitivity about its handling of race in the past: M. Roper, *Monkey See, Monkey Do: How Academia Turned Curious George into a Racial Commentary*, MA dissertation (University of Vermont, 2008). There is another, unnamed, white female museum scientist in later Curious George books – M. Rey and H. A. Rey, *Curious George's Dinosaur Discovery* (Boston, MA: Houghton Mifflin, 2006) – and in the Curious George stories produced in the more traditional illustrated style of Rey and Rey, which are still being issued in tandem with the PBS cartoonish tie-ins, there is a female museum director named Dr Lee – M. Rey and H. A. Rey, 'Curious George plants a tree' (2009), in M. Rey and H. A. Rey, *Curious George, Stories to Share* (Boston, MA: Houghton Mifflin Harcourt, 2011), p. 178 – although a white male museum director, in the style of the earlier guise of Professor Wiseman, appears in books too: M. Rey and H. A. Rey, *Curious George and the Dinosaur* (London: Walker, 2008).

[435] Wheelwright and Stimson, *Rollo's Journey to Cambridge*, p. 16

[436] Cory, *Little Jack Rabbit and The Squirrel Brothers* onwards.

[437] D. Cory, *Little Jack Rabbit and Professor Crow* (New York, NY: Grosset and Dunlap, 1922).

syndicated through newspapers on the East Coast of the United States[438] that owe much to *Br'er Rabbit*, published at the height of the Jim Crow laws that enforced racial segregation in America.[439] A blackbird called Jim Crow at this particular point in place and time,[440] depicted in this way, reinforces the 'romanticized version' of the stereotype of black people as 'simple and quaint, yet still irresponsible, stupid, and lazy'.[441] Another racist slur occurs in *Bugville Life for Big and Little Folk* with a disturbing pastoral ditty for preschoolers called 'Coon Songs in Bugville':

> Won't you teach me some coon songs, professor,
> Ere you flit from this garden aglow?
> All the critical bugs are aweary
> Of these ancient spring songs, don't you know.[442]

---

[438] For example, in Country Review, Syracuse, Friday, 28 March, 1921 (p. 19) or The Evening Journal, Wilmington, Delaware, Friday, 7 December, 1923 (p. 26).

[439] M. J. Klarman, *From Jim Crow to Civil Rights: The Supreme Court and the Struggle for Racial Equality* (Oxford: Oxford University Press, 2004).

[440] There is a blackbird called Jim Crow in L. F. Baum, *Policeman Bluejay* (Chicago, IL: The Reilly & Britton Co. Publishers, 1907), indicating that the example here is part of a longer tradition.

[441] F. Pratto, K. Henkel and I.-C. Lee, 'Stereotypes and prejudice from an intergroup relations perspective: their relation to social structure', in C. Stangor and C. S. Crandall, *Stereotyping and Prejudice* (New York, NY: Psychology Press, 2013), pp. 151–180, p. 172; see also E. Lott, *Love & Theft: Blackface Minstrelsy and the American Working Class* (Oxford University Press, 2013), p. 23 on black birds and Jim Crow, and M. Riggs, *Ethnic Notions: Black People in White Minds* (Berkeley, CA: California Newsreel, 1987), a documentary by Marlon Riggs that examines disturbing anti-black stereotypes which refuel anti-black prejudice.

[442] R. K. Munkittrick, G. Dirks and Judge Company, *Bugville Life for Big and Little Folk* (New York, NY: Judge Co., 1902), p. 38.

The dissonance between the ethnophaulism and the bucolic description is jarring, in a magazine with a readership of 65,000 children a month.[443] The earlier quote from Jack Dawe suggests the Western world viewpoint of "foreign" civilisations as "other" (see p. 72). These instances remind us that racial and political commentary can reverberate into stories written for children, teaching and reinforcing cultural and racial oppression: 'the colonising force of fiction to inculcate hegemonic ideologies or to reinforce gender roles is powerful through the history of children's literature.'[444]

The lack of ethnic diversity in these books mirrors the lack of diversity within academia itself.[445] In the United States in 2000, 72 % of faculty were white men, 17 % were white women, 8 % were men of colour

---

[443] P. Hutchinson, 'Harper's Young People and its rivals', *The Magazinist, Critical Thinking for Publishers* (2011), http://themagazinist.com/uploads/Harpers_Young_People.pdf.

[444] Thacker, 'Victorianism, empire and the paternal voice', p. 54. A recent response to this in adult fiction has been the rise of the postcolonial campus novel, 'highlighting the follies of academic life' while 'writing back to the empire': A. Mukhopadhyay, '"The Campus Novel in India is involved in elucidating a critique of post-liberalization middle-class culture" – a tête-à-tête with Amitabha Bagchi', *IUP Journal of English Studies*, 11(4), (2016), p. 124, www.iupindia.in/1612/English%20Studies/Interview_The_Campus_Novel.html; see also R. Sengupta, 'Campus Calling: The Curious Case of the "Campus Novel" in India', *Bookadda* (23 November 2012), http://blog.bookadda.com/campus-calling-the-curious-case-of-the-%E2%80%98campus-novel%E2%80%99-in-india/.

[445] See D. D. Bernal and O. Villalpando, 'An Apartheid of knowledge in academia: the struggle over the "legitimate" knowledge of faculty of color', *Equity and Excellence in Education*, 35(2), (2002), pp. 169–180 and D. Gabriel, 'Race, racism and resistance in British academia', in *Rassismuskritik und Widerstandsformen* (Springer Fachmedien Wiesbaden, 2017), pp. 493–505 for introductions.

and only 2 % were women of colour.[446] In the United Kingdom in 2015, 92.4 per cent of professors were white, with 0.49 % being black.[447] The trends observed here also follows those in children's publishing regarding ethnic diversity: only 4% of children's books published in the UK in 2017 featured BAME characters, despite 32% of pupils of compulsory school age in England being of minority ethnic origin,[448] and there being evidence to suggest that Black and Asian children – particularly girls – are those that both enjoy and are most regularly reading.[449] A rudimentary application of critical race theory[450] can aid us in understanding how problematic the lack of diversity is in both children's literature and the academy itself: which actors and processes can appropriate intellectual agency and authority, excluding others as they do so? Who is barred from both the real and the fictional professoriate, in structural and complicit decisions based on race? What affect does this cumulative lack of diversity and structural racism (a common criticism of children's literature) have on its readership?

[446] S. Y., Evans, 'Women of color in American higher education', *Thought & Action*, The NEA Higher Education Journal (Fall 2007), pp. 131–139, p. 131.

[447] C. E. Alexander and J. Arday, (eds.), *Aiming Higher: Race, Inequality and Diversity in the Academy* (Runnymede Trust, 2015), www.runnymedetrust.org/uploads/ Aiming%20Higher.pdf.

[448] Centre for Literacy in Primary Education (CLPE), 'Survey of Ethnic Representation within UK Children's Literature 2017' (2018) pp. 6–7 clpe.org.uk/ library-and-resources/research/reflecting-realities-survey-ethnic-representation-within-uk-children.

[449] C. Clark, 'Children's and Young People's Reading in 2014. Findings from the 2014 National Literacy Trust's annual survey', (National Literacy Trust, 2015) literacy trust.org.uk/research-services/research-reports/childrens-and-young-peoples-reading-2014.

[450] R. Delgado and J. Stefancic, *Critical Race Theory: An Introduction* (New York, NY: NYU Press, 2012).

4.6 *Visual Stereotypes and the Judging of Appearance: Age, Hair and Dress*

It is important that we unpack the visual stereotypes within the corpus, given that common media depictions of professors are

> of academics as mustachioed white men wearing tweed coats
> with elbow patches and doing their work in an office sur-
> rounded by books. Such assumptions are not only gendered
> masculine but have class, race, and heteronormative implica-
> tions as well.[451]

The academics are predominantly middle aged or older, classed by an interpretation of their appearance in illustrations. Six were smart children, most with
academic nicknames such as 'The Preschool Professors',[452] twenty-one were
young adults (aged 18–45), 128 were middle-aged (45–65) and 133 were elderly
(65+). Forty had indeterminate age (animals, spades, etc. – see Section 4.8).
However, it is worth noting that there were no elderly women: there are two
children, eight young adults, seventeen middle-aged and two indeterminately
aged females. There are no 'granny'-type females with white hair or any other
signifiers of age and experience. While this echoes

> the generational effect in the higher education and the govern-
> ment sectors, whereby women researchers, compared to men,

---

[451] A. A. Samek, and T. A. Donofrio, '"Academic Drag" and the performance of the
Critical Personae: an exchange on sexuality, politics, and identity in the academy',
Women's Studies in Communication, 36(1), (2013), 28–55, p. 46.

[452] Bale, *The Preschool Professors Learn How Seeds Grow.*

> are more concentrated in the youngest age groups, but the
> opposite is observed in the oldest age groups,[453]

it would also seem to indicate an impossibility that elderly woman – who are routinely feared, patronised, dismissed and held in contempt in children's literature[454] – can even be allowed within the fictional academy.[455] The elderly make up the largest section of fictional academics (41 per cent), but the old here are only men.

The attire of the academics was surprisingly formal, given academia's real-life reputation for scruffiness.[456] Eighty-nine are in a suit, a further twenty-seven wear a suit with bowtie, with an additional five in shirt and tie. Forty-eight are wearing a lab coat, five of these with bowtie. Twenty-two are in formal academic regalia (one wearing a gown accompanied fetchingly with bovver boots).[457]

---

[453] European Commission, 'She Figures 2015', p. 61.

[454] J. Johnson, R. Slater and The Open University, *Ageing and Later Life* (London: Sage Publications, 1993), p. 60.

[455] Professor McGonagall in the *Harry Potter* series (Rowling, *Harry Potter and the Philosopher's Stone* onwards) would best qualify as a rare example of a respected senior female with authority and heft, although she is not illustrated and so does not feature in our analysis.

[456] R. Toor, 'Can't we be smart and look good, too?' Chronicle Review, *The Chronicle of Higher Education* (3 April 2009), http://chronicle.com/article/cant-we-be-smart look/9397, J. Wolff, 'Why do academics dress so badly?', Guardian Higher Education, Marginal Notes, *Guardian* (21 October 2014), www.theguardian.com/education/2014/oct/21/why-do-academics-dress-so-badly. At time of writing – February 2017 – the query, 'why do academics' is autocompleted in Google with 'use big words, write so badly, write' and 'dress so badly', suggesting this is a popular question to ask about the professoriate.

[457] Mrs Hatchett, Doctor of Literature, teacher of primary school pirates, and proto-academic-Tank-Girl in *The Pirate's Mixed-up Voyage*: 'She wore terrifying black

Figure 18 The alien Professor Dribble, incognito. In Kettle, *Professor Dribble* (p. 44). Illustrated by Melissa Webb. Used with kind permission from Melissa Webb and Macmillan Education Australia.

Sixteen are in a safari suit and eleven wear magician's robes. Five are in black tie with an additional five also sporting a top-hat. Four are in spacesuits, four in military uniform, two in medieval robes and two in formal court uniform. Five females are wearing dresses and two are in twin sets: a quarter of the women wear lab coats and a further quarter wear suits, but no women sport ties, bowties or top-hats (Professor Peabody in the Eagle[458] wears a range of clothing from ballgowns to spacesuits). Only three academics are dressed casually in sweatshirts, and six wear jeans. There are also two academics in raincoats, and one each in a bomber jacket, chef's whites, climbing gear, cloak, clown suit, medical scrubs, pyjamas, traditional Chinese clothing, and fairy, jester, wrestler's trunks and superhero costume. There are, of course, various animals, aliens and vegetables that do not have any garments (see Section 4.8). The majority of those wearing clothing think they are dressed for authority and business, although there is a *lot* of tweed going on, and the suits are often crumpled and threadbare, living up to the unkempt stereotype where formal attire has seen better days. For example, in the choose-your-own-adventure book *Professor Q's Mysterious Machine*:

> You look up – all the way up. Past his scuffed brown shoes, up his rumpled, stained, baggy plaid pants, about five feet of them, up his dusty pink shirt that's buttoned wrong, up his long, skinny neck, up his long, skinny face, up to his thick black hair sticking out in all directions.[459]

boots and a belt all studded with spikes. At one hip swung a brass chain and at the other, a rather dashing sabre. Over this ensemble she wore the gown and hood of a Doctor of Literature' (Mahy and Chamberlain, *The Pirate's Mixed-Up Voyage*, p. 60).

[458] Eagle, 'Dan Dare', 1(5), (London: Hulton Press, 12 May 1950b onwards).

[459] D. Fletcher Crow, *Professor Q's Mysterious Machine* (Elgin, IL: Chariot Books, 1982), p. 1. Used by kind permission of David C. Cook and Chariot Books.

Hairstyles are where the formalities end: intellect is demonstrated with dishev-elled and uncouth styling. Although fify-four have neat, short hair, with a further eight with fashionable short men's haircuts, forty-nine are decidedly scruffy, with a further twenty-one sporting long white spiky hair, mimicking Einstein, who had by the mid-twentieth century come to represent the arche-type of American Genius.[460] His, hair, in particular, presented a 'symbol of populist intelligence':[461] we see it visually referenced again and again in Professor Gamma,[462] Professor I. Q.,[463] Professor Poopypants,[464] Professor Bumblebrain,[465] Professor Dinglebat[466] and Professor Von Evil.[467] One alien, Professor Dribble, disguises himself as Albert Einstein, including the hairstyle and moustache, to go incognito on planet Earth (Figure 18).[468]

Eighty-four men are bald, symptomatic of the age-range of candidates, but many of those sport long unkempt hair tufts. There are a few outliers – dreadlocks, Princess Leia buns, snakes, very long straight hair, neat bobs for women – but for the most part, big, messy hair is the order of the day, for academic men and women alike (see The Lecturer in *Mahalia Mouse Goes to*

---

[460] A. Lecklider, *Inventing the Egghead, The Battle over Brainpower in American Culture* (Philadelphia, PA: University of Pennsylvania Press, 2013), pp. 59–68. When I became a Professor, one of my children said, 'But you can't be. You don't have big white hair and a white coat.'

[461] Ibid., p. 65.   [462] Hoyle and Hoyle, *The Frozen Planet of Azuron*.

[463] Simon and Kendrick, *Professor I. Q. Explores the Senses*.

[464] Pilkey, *Captain Underpants and the Perilous Plot of Professor Poopypants*.

[465] Robb, *Professor Bumblebrain's Bonkers Book on God*; see Figure 26.

[466] Noonan, *Professor Dinglebat and the Dynamic Dog De-Barker*.

[467] M. Chabon and J. Parker, *The Astonishing Secret of Awesome Man* (London: HarperCollins Children's Books, 2011); see Figure 27.

[468] P. Kettle, *Professor Dribble* (South Yarra: Get Real, Macmillan Education Australia Pty Ltd, 2011b).

College[469] and *Professor Blabbermouth*[470]). This is particularly the case for those found in the latter (recent) half of the corpus, providing a counterpoint to lab coats and suits: the informal clashes with the formal. Given that almost half the corpus is illustrated with black and white images, it is difficult to ascertain anything meaningful about hair colour, although ninety-two men (no women) have white hair, and twenty-one men (no women) have grey hair (meaning 44 per cent of the humans in the corpus are greying or white-haired men). Of those in colour, ginger is the most common shade (*Professor Sniff and the Lost Spring Breezes*,[471] The Lecturer in *Mahalia Mouse Goes to College*[472]) but there are also renegades sporting coiffures that are purple (Professor Med Yusa in *Professor Gylden Lox's Hair School*[473]), green (*Professor Rock Ltd*[474]) and blue (*Professor Blue: Top Secret Lab Journal*[475]), reflecting the different and outsider nature of these characters.

One hundred and seventeen (45 per cent of the humans) have facial hair, with moustaches being most common (sixty-two), then beards (forty-eight), side-burns (five) and a goatee (two). Beards also have a tendency to be messy (see The Professor in *Mistress Masham's Repose*,[476] the waist-long beard of The Professor in *Comet in Moominland*,[477] the leaf-incrusted beard of *Professor*

[469] Lithgow and Oleynikov, *Mahalia Mouse Goes to College*.

[470] N. Watts, *Professor Blabbermouth on the Moon* (London: Scholastic Children's Books, 1996).

[471] A. Shearer and T. Kenyon, *Professor Sniff and the Lost Spring Breezes* (London: Gollancz, 1996b).

[472] Lithgow and Oleynikov, *Mahalia Mouse Goes to College*.

[473] Brownfeather and Wright Group, *Professor Gylden Lox's Hair School*.

[474] B. J. Hatch Jr and D. J. Chatham, *Professor Rock Ltd* (Baltimore, MD: Shooting Star Editions, 2003).

[475] M. Laskar and J. Shipman Bonwich, *Professor Blue: Top Secret Lab Journal* (Montreal: Les Editions Lastcall, 2010).

[476] White, *Mistress Masham's Repose*. [477] Jansson, *Comet in Moominland*.

Potts[478] or Professor Perkin in *Winnie's Dinosaur Day*[479]), culturally echoing the unkempt beards of Victorian gentlemen of intellectual renown, such as Charles Darwin, Edward Lear and Alfred, Lord Tennyson. None of the academic women have facial hair.

There are no visible physical disabilities, and no behaviour that can be classed other than heteronormative. This lack of inclusion is simultaneously problematic while reminding us of the lack of diversity routinely shown in children's literature,[480] and unintentionally, or subconsciously, mirroring the lack of diversity within the academy.[481] Statistics for the proportion of academic staff that have physical disabilities, or are LGBTQ, are difficult to ascertain, as disclosure rates are assumed to be poor given existing prejudices within society: 4.6 per cent of UK academic staff disclosed their disability in 2016, whereas 70 per cet of staff did not disclose their sexual orientation.[482] There is no attempt to represent academics in any way rather than being heterosexual and able-bodied: yet again, children's literature misses the

[478] Wright and Chapman, *Professor Potts Meets the Animals in Africa*.

[479] V. Thomas and K. Paul, *Winnie's Dinosaur Day* (Oxford: Oxford University Press, 2012).

[480] M. Leicester and T. Shrigley-Wightman, *Special Stories for Disability Awareness: Stories and Activities for Teachers, Parents and Professionals* (Jessica Kingsley Publishers, 2007); E. H. Rowell, 'Missing! Picture books reflecting gay and lesbian families', *Young Children*, 62(3), (2007), p. 24.

[481] M. L. Vance (ed.), *Disabled Faculty and Staff in a Disabling Society: Multiple Identities in Higher Education* (Association on Higher Education and Disability, 2007); E. V. Patridge, R. S. Barthelemy and S. R. Rankin, 'Factors impacting the academic climate for LGBQ STEM faculty', *Journal of Women and Minorities in Science and Engineering*, 20(1), (2014), pp. 75–98.

[482] The Equality Challenge Unit, 'Equality in Higher Education: Staff Statistical Report 2016' (2016), www.ecu.ac.uk/publications/equality-in-higher-education-statistical-report-2016/.

opportunity to address and tackle prejudices through positive representation of difference here, while both reflecting (and possibly critiquing?) the academy we have. The representation of mental health issues is discussed in Section 5.

4.7 Class

It is worth looking at 'what kinds of economic lives are presented as *normal* and therefore *desirable*' in these books.[483] Although there is only one Lord,[484] the message is projected over and again that academia is associated with wealth (particularly in the books produced in the United Kingdom). Academic homes are very different from those of the average reader: for example, the mansions of Professor Digory Kirke,[485] Professor Diggins,[486] Doktor Bunsen Van Der Dunkel's ancient, lonely castle,[487] Dr Monsoon Taggert, who planned to build a palace but it came out as a very large mansion,[488] Professor Quickly[489] and Doctor Harleyson.[490] Professor Sniff lives on a huge wind farm, and a point is made of the 'parents' small flat' of the children who befriend him.[491] We've already covered all the servants, housekeepers and cooks. In addition, the top hats and tails sported by some academics project class privilege, but so do displays of disposable income. Professors have hobbies that require vast

---

[483] S. Jones, 'Grass houses: representations and reinventions of social class through children's literature', *Journal of Language and Literacy Education*, 4(2), (2008), 40–58, p. 43.

[484] Asriel, in Pullman, *Northern Lights*.

[485] Lewis, *The Lion, the Witch and the Wardrobe*.

[486] Holman, Ohlsson, Valen and Valen, *Professor Diggins' Dragons*.

[487] Ungerer, *Moon Man*, p. 26.

[488] A. Matthews, *Dr Monsoon Taggert's Amazing Finishing Academy* (London: Mammoth, Methuen Children's Books Limited, 1990), p. 70.

[489] C. Harris and M. Hingley, *Professor Quickly* (Oxford: Oxford University Press, 1993).

[490] Cassels, *The Mysterious Collection of Dr David Harleyson*.

[491] Shearer and Kenyon, *Professor Sniff and the Lost Spring Breezes*, p. 2.

resources, such as designing their own hot-air balloons.[492] The Professor in *Babar and the Professor* has enough wealth to design and build a river boat massive enough to transport many elephant friends, on a whim.[493] The unnamed palaeontologist in *The Dog That Dug* can quickly rustle up a fortune to purchase the bones of an unearthed dinosaur fossil:

> 'Look here,' said the prof, 'I'm not being funny,
> Give me those bones and I'll give you some money.'
> 'Great!' said the dog, holding out one of his paws,
> 'Two million pounds and the bones will be yours!'
> The prof scratched her head and went 'Um . . .' and 'Ah . . .'
> Then paid him in cash and put the bones in her car.[494]

There is also discussion of expensive possessions. Packing a picnic for her Professor husband,

> Mrs Diggins . . . had fitted a small cupboard with cups and dishes, silverware and linens. 'You may wish to rough it' she said, 'but sometimes you may tire of that and wish to use some nice china and silver'. So she put in a set of her good Meissen, packing it carefully, and some handsome silverware and a good damask cloth.[495]

To finance a trip to the moon, Professor Blabbermouth 'sold everything – all Blabbermouth's valuable oil paintings, her stocks and shares, even her shoes

---

[492] G. Timmermans, *The Great Balloon Race* (London: Methuen, 1976); H. C. Andersen, J. Hersholt, N. Daniel and A. Disl, *The Fairy Tales of Hans Christian Andersen* (Hohenzollernting, Köln, Germany: Taschen GmbH, 2013).

[493] L. de Brunhoff and O. Jones, *Babar and the Professor* (London: Methuen Children's Books, 1972).

[494] Long and Paul, *The Dog that Dug*, pp. 23–24.

[495] Holman, Ohlsson, Valen and Valen, *Professor Diggins' Dragons*, p. 17. Used by kind permission of Felice Holman.

and socks'.[496] These fortunes are not immutable: Professor Digory Kirke's 'very large house'[497] is lost by *The Voyage of the Dawn Treader* as 'he had somehow become poor since the old days and was living in a small cottage with only one bedroom to spare'[498] – the shame of it! – and The Professor in *Mistress Masham's Repose* was 'as poor as a church mouse'[499] and frequently starving. However, clues abound that the professoriat is upper middle class, if not upper class, with wealth, comfort and disposable income, giving clear messages out to the readership of their social and economic standing, presenting a further barrier between them and the majority of child readers. This, of course, is reflected in the real-life academy, which follows a 'steeply hierarchical structure that reflects profound social inequality',[500] with entrenched 'practices of class elitism and discrimination'[501] contributing to 'negative perceptions of the university',[502] which has resulting impacts that further compound class

---

[496] Watts, *Professor Blabbermouth on the Moon*, p. 17. Used by kind permission of David Higham Associates.

[497] Lewis *The Lion, the Witch and the Wardrobe*, p. 1.

[498] Lewis, *The Voyage of the Dawn Treader*, p. 8. VOYAGE OF THE DAWN TREADER by C. S. Lewis © copyright CS Lewis Pte Ltd 1952. Used by kind permission.

[499] White, *Mistress Masham's Repose*, p. 17. © T. H. White, and G. P. Putnam and Sons. Used by kind permission of Random House Children's Publishers and David Higham Associates.

[500] A. Clauset, S. Arbesman and D. B. Larremore, 'Systematic inequality and hierarchy in faculty hiring networks', *Science Advances*, 1(1), (2015), DOI: 10.1126/sciadv.1400005, http://advances.sciencemag.org/content/1/1/e1400005.full, p. 1.

[501] D. Reay, 'Social class in UK higher education: still an elephant in the room', in J. Cote and A. Furlong (eds.), *Routledge Handbook of the Sociology of Higher Education* (Abingdon: Routledge, 2016), pp 131–141, p. 132.

[502] S. Baars, E. Mulcahy and E. Bernardes, *The Underrepresentation of White Working Class Boys in Higher Education: The Role of Widening Participation* (London: King's

inequalities, for example, in low uptake in higher education attendance from working-class students, particularly white boys,[503] while apparently 'only the rich can afford to work at Oxford and Cambridge'.[504] We have, at some point, to consider how stereotypes of academia are linked to current realities, and the effect this will have on an audience, and shall do so in Section 6.

4.8 Not All Fictional Academics are Created Human

Although 260 (79 per cent) of the fictional academics are human, there are other forms of Professor or Doctor. Forty-five (14 per cent) are animals: with six dogs, five mice, three cats, two toads, two frogs and an ant, bandicoot, bear, beaver, beetle, chimp, chipmunk, cockatoo, cockroach, crow, dumbo octopus, gorilla, kingfisher, lion, mole, monkey, otter, owl, pig, porcupine, possum, rabbit, rat, rhino, rooster, shark and stegosaurus. This does not seem to correlate with any dominance of stereotypical representation of intellectual anthropomorphism (such as Athena's owl, or wily foxes); however, it sits within a long history of animal and object stories that help us query 'our own species' . . . claim to distinction'.[505] This also ventures into the Lacanian

College London, 2016), www.lkmco.org/wp-content/uploads/2016/07/The-underrepresentation-of-white-working-class-boys-in-higher-education-baars-et-al-2016.pdf, p. 1.

[503] Ibid.

[504] Guardian Higher Education Network, 'Only the rich can afford to work at Oxford and Cambridge', Academics Anonymous, Friday, 20 November 2015, www.theguardian.com/higher-education-network/2015/nov/20/only-the-rich-can-afford-to-work-at-oxford-and-cambridge.

[505] D. Rudd, 'Animal and object stories', in M. O. Grenby and A. Immel (eds), *Cambridge Companion to Children's Literature* (Cambridge University Press, 2009), pp. 242–257, p. 245.

Symbolic, conferring animated life in 'an anti-Cartesian world where animism rules, where all things are democratically, anarchically, even, given a voice':[506] the corpus has five aliens, and one each of centaur, comic book bubble, fairy, gorgon, half-human half-dwarf, half-human half-giant, mineral, sock, spade and vegetable.[507] These representations challenge the intellectual authority and importance of academics, and intellectuals can be reduced to caricature: if a rock can be a professor, what value does the title give?[508] The symbolic representations are also heavily gendered with easily identifiable traits that reflect and reinforce societal conventions. Only two are female: Mahalia Mouse[509] and Professor Steg the Stegosaurus in *Fortunately, the Milk* ...[510] Even four of the five academics who are godlike omniscient narrators, not pictured themselves, have male gender-specific traits and pronouns. The teacher's guide to *Fortunately, the Milk...*, provided by Bloomsbury, asks, 'Were you surprised to learn that Professor Steg is female? If so, why?'[511]

4.9 Academic Title

The majority of academics in the corpus are professors (259, 80 per cent) with forty-two doctors. There are eight university students, two researchers, two lecturers, two heads of college and various administrators, a chancellor, a vice-warden, a keeper of a museum, a research assistant and personal assistant combined, a post-doc and, in what is probably the most specific university-

---

[506] Ibid., p. 248.

[507] (*Professor Peabody* – get it?) G. Reed, *Professor Peabody*, A Munch Bunch Book (Ipswich: Studio Publications (Ipswich) Limited, 1979).

[508] Hatch and Chatham, *Professor Rock Ltd.*

[509] Lithgow and Oleynikov, *Mahalia Mouse Goes to College.*

[510] N. Gaiman and C. Riddell, *Fortunately, the Milk...* (London: Bloomsbury, 2013).

[511] Bloomsbury, *Teachers' Guide to 'Fortunately, the Milk...' by Neil Gaiman and Chris Riddell* (London: Bloomsbury, n. d.), https://media.bloomsbury.com/rep/files/fortunately-the-milk-teacher-notes.pdf, p. 4.

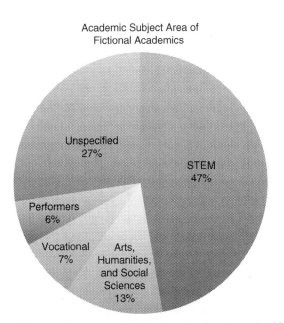

Chart 4 Subject area of fictional academics, determined by mention of subject within text.

related book title of a children's text ever, an *Assistant Professor Toad* who is a 'not-so-smart snozzie scientist from the Snoz Invention Centre, and he was EXTREMELY jealous of Professor Dribble'.[512] It is debateable whether these

[512] P. Kettle, *Assistant Professor Toad* (South Yarra: Get Real, Macmillan Education Australia Pty Ltd, 2011a), p. 9. Used by kind permission of The McGraw-Hill Companies, Inc.

roles would be understood by their audience, especially given that they usually appear without explanation or backstory. The fact that most academics are represented with the most senior of titles – where are all the students? – creates distance between them and the childhood audience of the books, setting an unknown and unnamed process of how one would acquire this honorific between character and reader.[513] The fictional characters form representations of intellectual achievement that are not a known continuum of a child's own schooling, but another, strange authority: separate and unexplained, as Lithgow commented, they are 'very, very, far away'.[514]

4.10 Academic Subject Area

Science, Technology, Engineering and Mathematics (STEM) dominate the subject area of fictional academics (Chart 4).

Although eighty-nine (27 per cent of) fictional academics have no subject area specifically linked to them (this includes the six children), 154 (47 per cent) are specifically linked to STEM areas, with fifty-four scientists, twenty-three inventors, thirteen zoologists, ten biologists, seven mathematicians, six medical researchers, four chemists, five palaeontologists, three astronomers and two each of engineers, physicists and rocket scientists. There is one aeronaut, astrophysicist, botanist, computing scientist, ecologist, explorer, geographer, geologist, marine biologist, oceanographer,

---

[513] The explorer father in the Maisie books seems to progress through academic titles, although this is not fully explained (see footnote 341). Although it may seem that Dr Xargle gets promoted to Professor Xargle over the course of the series of books in which he is featured (Willis and Ross, *Dr Xargle's Book of Earthlets* onwards), this is actually due to the difference between the British and American editions, reflecting different usage of the title of Professor in the United States and subsequent repackaging of books to reflect that.

[514] Lithgow, 'Actor John Lithgow Discusses Mahalia Mouse Goes to College'.

criminal scientist, space scientist, veterinary scientist, metereologist, natural historian, psychologist and food scientist. Getting into the questionable areas of 'science', there is also a homeopath and a Necrobioneopalaeonthydrochthonanthropopithekologist (showing the ineffectual and questionable science of Professor Ptthmllnsprts in *The Water Babies*[515]). Five are in non-existent mythical beast 'subjects', with three in Dragonology or Serpentology (studying Dragons), one researching Unicorns and one undertaking the very scary-sounding 'demonological research' (Professor Van Helsing in *How to Slay a Werewolf*[516]). This indicates a small attempt to take science and academic authority into the mythological, imaginative realm.

There are only eighty-four (26 per cent) who are non-STEM, and although they represent a wide range of experience and expertise, this bias towards the sciences projects a very limited picture of the subject range that is available, and important to children, at university level. This, of course, is a battle fought by the Arts, Humanities and Social Sciences for government funds, for a fair representation of the way universities are presented in the media and even for fair support within institutions,[517] but it is worrying that it is also played out in children's books, suggesting entrenched cultural biases regarding the academic value of non-STEM areas.[518] The interests of non-

---

[515] Kingsley, *The Water-Babies*. [516] Howard and Walker, *How to Slay a Werewolf*.

[517] American Academy of Arts and Sciences 2013; see also M. Terras, E. Priego, A. Liu et al., 'The Humanities Matter!' Infographic (2013), http://4humanities.org/2013/07/the-humanities-matter-infographic/.

[518] The children's TV show *Sesame Street* has realised this problematic focus on one aspect of education. It has pledged from Season 43 (2012–13) that, while it will continue 'its focus on STEM education' it will add 'the arts to the equation, creating STEAM. The cornerstone of the curriculum remains the connection between the four main domains: science, technology, engineering and mathematics, but the

STEM experts can be divided into three areas: the Humanities and Social Sciences (13 %), Performing Arts (6 %) and vocational subjects (7 %). Within the Humanities and Social Sciences, the most common subject areas as archaeology (nine), history (five), museology (five), music (five), linguistics (four), education studies (four), economics (two), with one in anthropology, art, Chinese, literature, manuscript studies, psychology, theatre, theology and religion. The vocational cluster has fourteen teachers, two hairdressers, two cooks and one each of an administrator, explorer, headteacher, secret agent, comic book artist and vocal instructor. The performing arts cluster has twelve magicians and entertainers, one clown and a downright fraudster. Interestingly, this shows a non-university influence within children's illustrated literature: the Music Hall, presenting the professor as entertainer rather than scientist, which will be explored below in Section 4.11.

Women are not necessarily associated with the 'softer' academic subjects. Granted, there is a hairdresser, and four that undertake more traditional Arts and Humanities subject areas (a doctor of literature, a student of history, an anthropologist and an archaeologist) and a teacher, which have been subjects traditionally more statistically likely to be chosen by females than males;[519] however, there are also four female scientists, two palaeontologists, two museum scientists and a botanist, chemist, ecologist, engineer, economist, mathematician, physicist, one

updated approach integrates the arts. This helps make learning STEM concepts relevant and enticing to young children by highlighting how artists use STEM knowledge to enhance their art or solve problems. It also provides context for the importance of STEM knowledge in careers in the arts (e.g. musician, painter, sculptor and dancer)': Sesame Workshop, 'Stem + A = Steam. When art meets science, technology, engineering and math' (2012), www.sesameworkshop.org/season43/about-the-show/curriculum/.

[519] B. Zafar, 'College major choice and the gender gap', *Journal of Human Resources*, 48 (3), (2013), 545–595.

who studies dragons and another who studies unicorns. The few women who do appear are often wonderful role models, for example, the fictional author of *My First Pet Dragon: The Complete Handbook for Beginners*:

> Professor Georgie Blink (BSc, MSc, PhD, Dip. Drag, OBE), studied at London University, Harvard, and the Centre for Advanced Dragon Studies in Vladivostock. She is a world expert in dragons, and a founding member of the International College of Serpentology. She now lives near Bristol, England, with an 85 year old Stumptailed Bolonka dragon called Picton. The professor has kept dragons since childhood and is a regular contributor to many dragon owner helplines and newsletters. The Professor and Picton are available for occasional visits to well-fireproofed schools.[520]

The fact that 27 per cent of the academics do not have any subject area at all is interesting: indicating that that characterisation is about expertise and authority, without necessarily displaying that in any way beyond the character's own interactions with those around them. This is particularly the case with non-human academics, for example, the spade in *Traction Man is Here*:[521] 'wicked professor spade is really just a spade with a name – (what on earth is it going to be a professor of?)'.[522] The honorific titles add meaning by linking to

---

[520] A. Mitchison (ed.), *My First Pet Dragon: The Complete Handbook for Beginners* (London: Catnip Books, 2008), p. i. Used by kind permission of the author and LAW Writers and Artists' Agents.

[521] M. Grey, *Traction Man is Here* (London: Cape Children's, 2005).

[522] Grey, personal communication, February 2017.

stereotypical prior associations of how doctors and professors behave, without necessarily positioning them in an area of expertise.

4.11 Puppeteers, Magicians and Performers

Throughout the corpus, there is prevailing influence of the academic as entertainer. Before the growth of the university sector and the establishment of academia as a profession in the late nineteenth century, mock honorifics and grandiose titles were assumed to denote expertise in music halls and circuses. Punch and Judy men had been called Professors since the eighteenth century.[523] By 1864 it was noted that the word 'professor' was 'so desecrated in its use that we are most familiar with it in connection with dancing schools, juggler's booths, and veterinary surgeries',[524] and during this period the term 'professor' was 'commonly adopted by marionette players, band directors, animal trainers, magicians, ventriloquists, acrobats, etc'.[525] Wilson writes of Victorian animal trainers using honorifics, including the sea lion tamer Professor, or Captain, Woodward[526] and the dog trainers Professor Chard and Professor Devereaux.[527] The conjuror George Arthur Fox took on his stage name Professor De Lyle 'from a tin of Lyle's Golden Syrup, adding De for a touch of class and gave himself the title of Professor, as all good Punch and Judy men are called'.[528] The

[523] R. Howard, *Punch and Judy in 19th Century America: A History and Biographical Dictionary* (McFarland, 2013), p. 43.

[524] J. H. Burton, *The Scot Abroad*, volume 1 (Edinburgh: Blackwood, 1864), p. 255.

[525] Howard, *Punch and Judy in 19th Century America*, p. 43.

[526] D. A. Wilson, 'Sea lions, greasepaint and the U-boat threat: Admiralty scientists turn to the music hall in 1916', *Notes and Records of The Royal Society*, 55(3), (2001), pp. 425–455.

[527] D. A., Wilson, *The Welfare of Performing Animals: A Historical Perspective* (Springer, 2015), p. 28.

[528] D. Monks, *The Magical De Lyles. Professor De Lyle, The Sheffield Conjuror with the Pocketful of Sixpences. By Grandson David W. Monks* (Self-published, 2017), p. 1.

usage of the term in this way fell out of favour in the second quarter of the twentieth century.[529] However, we see the echoes of these showmen, in both subject area and dress: white-tied, top-hatted and ready to dazzle. The earliest example is Professor Wolley Cobble:

> My occasional neighbour, Mr Cobble – or, as he delights in being called, 'PROFESSOR WOLLEY-COBBLE' – always draws a good audience when he exhibits his Peep-Show in Piccadilly or in Regent Street. He is of the old school of Showmen: voluble in small talk, ever ready with answers to countrymen and others, and with a never-ending supply of Bartholomew Fair trumpet-jokes.[530]

He is followed by Professor Knox,

> A famous professor who works a cat and dog show . . . who had just arrived in town from circuit. He was a Professor. A what? In the public business, had a caravan and worked dogs and cats.[531]

Professor Bolero 'Cannon Ball Tosser and Lightning Change Artist to the Crowned Heads of Europe', asks:

---

[529] OED Online, 'professor, n.' [530] *Walk Up! Walk Up!*, p. 1.
[531] C. R. Morley and L. Wain, *Peter, a Cat o' One Tail: His Life and Adventures* (New York, NY: G. P. Putnam's Sons, 1892), p. 50.

> I'm a poor man, sir, with a large family, sir, an' I'd be very
> thankful for any small jobs, sir, like givin' you sparrin' lessons,
> or massage, or takin' care of the furnace, sir![532]

Tom Sawyer, Huck Finn and Jim join The Professor, a showman with a balloon in *Tom Sawyer Abroad*:

> He has a good enough sort of a cretur, and hadn't no harm in him,
> and was just a genius, as the papers said, which wasn't his fault.
> We can't all be sound: we've got to be the way we are made.[533]

These figures are often sinister, and linked to magic, money-making and then on to fraud.[534] For example, Professor de Lara in *The Twopenny Spell* (Figure 19):

> She looked for the name over the shop. Instead of being some-
> body or other, Florist, it was 'Dolor de Lara, Professor of white
> and black Magic,' and in the window was a large card, framed
> and glazed. It said:

---

[532] A. B. Frost, *The Bull Calf and Other Tales* (London: J. C. Nimmo, 1892), pp. 83–4.

[533] Twain, *Tom Sawyer Abroad*, p. 22. A similar character is found in H. C. Andersen, 'The Flea and the Professor', *Scribner's Monthly*, 5(6), (April 1873), pp. 759–761, although this character is not illustrated until much later; see Andersen, Hersholt, Daniel and Disl, *The Fairy Tales of Hans Christian Andersen*.

[534] In the adventure story by J. T. Trowbridge, 'His own master', *St Nicholas*, IV(3), (January 1877), pp. 171–178, the term 'professor' is used throughout as a common noun, suggesting a type of behaviour from a vagabond, rather than a proper noun specifying any social standing or qualification. In McLoughlin Bros, inc., *The Monkeys Circus*, *Circus Stories* (New York, NY: McLoughlin Brothers New-York, 1883) the term is used for a group of musicians.

ENCHANTMENTS DONE WHILE YOU WAIT. EVERY DESCRIPTION OF CHARM CAREFULLY AND COMPETENTLY WORKED. STRONG SPELLS FROM FIFTY GUINEAS TO TWO PENCE. WE SUIT ALL PURSES. GIVE US A TRIAL. BEST AND CHEAPEST HOUSE IN THE TRADE.[535]

De Lara tricks Lucy into buying a spell that will make her strong, and her brother weak ("'No goods exchanged," he said crossly; "you've got what you asked for"'[536]), although the children's one-day switching of roles leads to better behaviour from both, long-term.

The circus and music hall echo throughout the corpus, in *The Highly Trained Dogs of Professor Petit*,[537] *Dr Merlin's Magic Shop*,[538] Professor Ali Pokanini, 'musician, magician, ventriloquist, and imitator' in *The Four Adventurers meet The Evil Professor*[539] and the magician Dr Sanders in *Rupert and the Rope Trick*.[540] *Professor Fergus Fahrenheit* blends the conman and scientist together with *His Wonderful Weather Machine*,[541] in a fictionalised story of the travelling rainmakers that would fraudulently extort money for precipitation spells in the Great Plains

[535] Nesbit, 'The twopenny spell', p. 169. [536] Ibid., p. 171.

[537] C. Ryrie Brink and R. Henneberger, *The Highly Trained Dogs of Professor Petit* (New York, NY: Scholastic Book Services, 1953).

[538] S. Corbett and J. Mathieu, *Dr Merlin's Magic Shop* (Boston: Little, Brown, 1973).

[539] P. Prins, *The Four Adventurers Meet the Evil Professor* (St Catherines, ON: Paideia Press, 1980), p. 132.

[540] N. Redfern, *Rupert and the Rope Trick in Your Favourite Rupert Story Collection* (London: Dean, 1993a).

[541] C. Groth-Fleming and D. Weller, *Professor Fergus Fahrenheit and His Wonderful Weather Machine* (New York, NY: Simon & Schuster Books for Young Readers, 1994).

' " And what can we do for you to-day, Miss ?" '—Page 170.

Figure 19 Professor de Lara in Nesbit, 'The twopenny spell', from *Oswald Bastable and Others*. Illustrated by Charles E. Brock. Public Domain: image from copy held in Osmania University Library, available via Digital Library of India, from archive.org. This is a busy street: someone must have seen them.

states.[542] Professor Gilderoy Lockhart in *Harry Potter and the Chamber of Secrets* is unmasked as a fraud, after building his celebrity on unfounded public bragging.[543] There is also a long-established cultural link to magic and performance as science, inherited from the trope of the alchemist,[544] which plays out in this suggestion of science and intellect as magic; for example, the long-lived scientist, Doktor Bunsen van der Dunkel in *Moon Man*,[545] who had been trying to build a spacecraft to fly to the moon for hundreds of years, is shown, now, as the bald-headed elderly lab-coated scientist surrounding by electronic equipment, standing in front of a portrait of his younger self as a wizard.[546] The professor as performer and magician, inherited from circus and music hall traditions and linked to the coinciding representation of scientist as alchemist, is therefore an important trope that lives on in children's literature, long after the music halls themselves have closed.[547]

---

[542] See J. Townsend, *Making Rain in America: A History* (Lubbock, TX: International Center for Arid and Semi-Arid Land Studies, Texas Tech University, 1975) for the history of rainmaking in America.

[543] Rowling, *Harry Potter and the Chamber of Secrets*.

[544] See Haynes, *From Faust to Strangelove*, pp. 9–22.

[545] Ungerer, *Moon Man*, p. 28.

[546] It was my six-year-old, Ferg, who pointed this out.

[547] This influence can be found in other enduring works of children's literature: Lerer, *Children's Literature*, p. 32 describes Roald Dahl's Willy Wonka as 'a blend of Captain Hook, circus ringmaster, puppeteer, and mad scientist'. There is direct, literal crossover between magic and Professors embodied in the teachers of Hogwarts School of Witchcraft and Wizardry (Rowling, *Harry Potter and the Philosopher's Stone* onwards).

4.12 The Academics in the Plot

There is little use made of characters' intellectual expertise. Academics tend to function in a similar way to the childlike, childless 'avuncular older men'[548] trope who shift the balance between adults and children, no longer being 'the bringers of discipline or wisdom'.[549] Many of the benevolent, baffled professors interact with children and 'themselves learned from, and were liberated by, the children'.[550] Plots are usually spurred on by children coming into contact with these lone, family-less, eccentric academics, allowing interactions which usually occur without parental supervision or input: the agent acting *in loco parentis* exhibiting behaviour far removed from typical familial activity. These interactions can take two forms, the first in an extension of the Jungian 'wise old man'[551] trope in children's literature where the professor passes on wisdom that extends and challenges the child's normality. For example, the Pevensie children in *The Lion, The Witch and the Wardrobe* are 'sent away from London during the War because of the air-raids' to the home of Professor Digory Kirke (Figure 20),[552] who is no relation to them, persuading them of the logic that parallel worlds exist:

> 'Nothing is more probable,' said the Professor, taking off his spectacles and beginning to polish them, while he muttered to himself, 'I wonder what they do teach them at these schools'.[553]

Lydia and Jarmes McGill (sic) are educated in wider possibilities of the natural world in *Professor Diggins' Dragons*:

---

[548] Grenby, *Children's Literature*, p. 128. [549] Ibid. [550] Ibid.
[551] Jung, *Collected Works of C. G. Jung*, Vol. 9, Part 1, 2nd ed.
[552] Lewis, *The Lion, the Witch and the Wardrobe*, p. 1. [553] Ibid., p. 49.

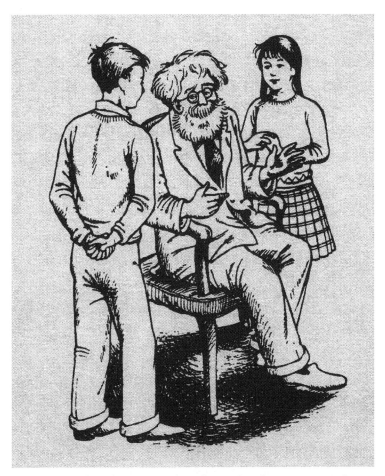

Figure 20 Professor Digory Kirke in his study advising Peter and Susan Pevensie, in Lewis, *The Lion, The Witch and the Wardrobe* (1950, p. 49). Illustration by Pauline Baynes, © Copyright CS Lewis Pte Ltd 1950. Used with permission.

> [I]t was part of their daily life to walk with the Professor on their way to school, and on *his* way to the University, and at that time to hear stories and riddles and songs and ideas about all manner of things that were exciting enough to carry them through spelling and arithmetic and well into civics.[554]

The reader in the biblical choose-your-own-adventure *Professor Q's Mysterious Machine* visits Professor Quinten to return a book, ending up in a time machine witnessing (and perhaps dying in) various battles that feature in the scriptures, learning more about Jesus in the process.[555] The wise old man in these books opens up the world to the children. A child next door helps explore *The Professor's Garden* in Maclennan: 'My mom said the Professor's garden was a mess. But he liked it that way, and so did I'.[556] The death of the Professor next door means the child has to process loss, and understand the importance of acts of remembrance, for a friend who had engaged with glee in the child's games (Figure 21).

An inversion of this is where the child's interaction changes the academic's thinking by challenging their scientific values. Giddens notes that cultures of illustration in didactic children's books of the Victorian period were 'surprisingly reluctant to represent the child engaging with science' but that fantasy such as Kingsley's *The Water-Babies* 'inaugurated a tradition of visually representing the child scientist (or at the very least the inquisitive child) – leading to the possibility of the child engaging

---

[554] Holman, Ohlsson, Valen and Valen, *Professor Diggins' Dragons*, pp. 1–2.

[555] Fletcher Crow, *Professor Q's Mysterious Machine*.

[556] B. Maclennan, *The Professor's Garden* (Cape Town: Songlono Books, David Philip Publishers, 1993), p. 1. Used by kind permission of New Africa Books.

Figure 21 Katy and her friendship with her 'eccentric old neighbour' who sports academic robes while scaring starlings, in Maclennan, *The Professor's Garden* (p. 10). Illustrated by Elizabeth Andrew. Used with permission, New Africa Books.

critically with the natural and mechanical world'.[557] Professor Ptthmllnsprts in *The Water-Babies*[558] is a friend sent out to look for biological specimens on a seaside walk, to educate an estate owner's daughter, Ellie (Figure 22):

> For in the stupid old times, you must understand, children were taught to know one thing, and to know it well; but in these enlightened new times they are taught to know a little about everything, and to know it all ill; which is a great deal pleasanter and easier, and therefore quite right ... So Ellie and he were walking on the rocks, and he was showing her about one in ten thousand of all the beautiful and curious things which are to be seen there ... Now little Ellie was, I suppose, a stupid little girl; for, instead of being convinced by Professor Ptthmllnsprts' arguments, she only asked the same question over again. 'But why are there not water-babies?'[559]

They come across Tom, the Water-Baby, and Ellie's childhood views challenge Ptthmllnsprts' scientific approach, eventually sending him mad. *The Water-Babies* is closely linked to, and satirises, real scientific debates and characters of the period (which Kingsley was enmeshed in), but also sets up the fictional academic in children's literature as ineffectual with a tendency towards insanity. Although a relatively minor character in the book,

---

[557] Giddens, 'Ptthmllnsprts: Visualising Science in Nineteenth-Century Children's Fantasy'.

[558] Kingsley, *The Water-Babies*. [559] Kingsley, *The Water*-Babies, 1885, pp. 169–176.

Figure 22 Professor Ptthmllnsprts walking alone with Ellie at the seaside, in the 1915 edition of Kingsley, *The Water-Babies*, illustrated by W. Heath Robinson, p. 136. Note that he is also holding a book, signalling expertise. Public Domain: Image from copy held at New York Public Library, scanned by Nicole Deyo, available at archive.org.

Ptthmllnsprts was (and is)[560] experienced by a very broad audience, promoting a sense of ridiculousness and failure associated with experts and intellectual achievement[561] while also establishing the child as essential foil to academic expertise.

The primary school-aged Finn in *The Rooftop Rocket Party* 'went to visit Doctor Gass in New York. Doctor Gass was a famous rocket scientist',[562] although he keeps his rockets only 'in the most secret and unusual place of all ... my *head*!!'[563] Finn ends up educating him about the presence of the 'unmathematical ... so very unscientific' man in the moon;[564] The botanist Professor Tobin takes a room in Maisie Hitchin's Grandmother's boarding house in *The Case of the Feathered Mask*,[565] allowing Maisie to solve the mystery of a theft that the adults cannot comprehend. This mechanism links the trope of the 'wise old man' to the trope of the wise or 'divine child' (the romantic motif where 'the adult moves from teacher to student, from stern moralizing to the

---

[560] Much has been made about the falling sales of, and current disinterest in, Kingsley, *The Water-Babies* – for example, D. Stevenson, 'Sentiment and significance: the impossibility of recovery in the children's literature canon, or The Drowning of The Water-Babies', *The Lion and the Unicorn*, 21(1), (1997), 112–130 – although no statistical analysis has underpinned this assumption.

[561] Parodoxically, Tom's reward for his trials in Kingsley, *The Water-Babies* is to become 'a great man of science, and can plan railroads, and steam-engines, and electric telegraphs, and rifled guns, and so forth; and knows everything about everything' (Kingsley, *The Water-Babies*, 1915, p. 316), suggesting that Kingsley's view on academia were nuanced, and he thought the practical aspects were to be celebrated.

[562] R. Chambers, *The Rooftop Rocket Party* (London: Andersen, 2002), p. 1. Used with permission, Andersen Press.

[563] Ibid., p. 14.   [564] Ibid., p. 28.

[565] Webb, *Maisie Hitchins: The Case of the Feathered Mask*.

undisciplined child to patient listening to the wise instruction of the simple and imaginative child',[566] another Jungian motif). The academic figures can 'constitute alternative ideals for children.[567] They stand as figures for the father, for the writer, for the adult authority in society'[568] but also represent what happens when this authority fails. This plays with intellectual agency, questioning expertise, prestige and power, and the child's place in social constructs, while also indicating room for intellectual aspiration and potential, alternative, pathways to adulthood. However, these traits are taken to extremes in the stereotypes discussed in the following section, as academics become so baffled as to be ineffectual, or so eccentric as to be mad and dangerous.

4.13 Conclusion: The Stereotypes Emerge

Undertaking a content analysis of this corpus of 289 books has allowed the dominant visual stereotype of an academic, particularly in the latter part of the twentieth century, to emerge: a professor in children's literature is now generally an elderly white able-bodied scruffy man with sticking-out messy hair and perhaps an unruly beard. The related texts suggest that they are most likely to be a scientist or inventor, with wealth or at least disposable income, and have a support network of wife or housekeeper to aid and assist them. They are most likely to be depicted away from the university, either at home or on some form of trip. It is these characters that are the most important part in children's literature, rather than the universities or

---

[566] D. Sandner, *The Fantastic Sublime: Romanticism and Transcendence in Nineteenth-Century Children's Fantasy Literature* (Westport, CT and London: Greenwood Publishing Group, 1996), p. 8.

[567] Jung, *Collected Works of C. G. Jung*, Vol. 9, Part 1, 2nd ed, p 161

[568] Lerer, *Children's Literature*, p. 149.

institutions that they belong to: 'academics act as a symbol for higher education in popular culture'.[569] There is little attention paid to fictional academics' work or expertise, rather than what they do when involved in the plot, often interacting in some way with children, playing with ideas of intellectual agency and power.

Throughout this analysis, the counts and statistics revealed have been related to available information regarding the diversity (or not) of academia. It is tempting to reflect that many of the books were written throughout the late nineteenth and into the middle of the twentieth century, and parallels that can be drawn indicate that, although the representation of academics within children's texts may be non-diverse and problematic, it may somewhat fairly reflect the real-world academy and wider socio-political structures as instantiated during that period. It would be too easy to discount these texts as being 'of their time'. With half of the corpus being written after 1993, many of the representations we see have chosen to self-refer to established tropes and stereotypes, indicating that that the cultural hegemony continues in modern society and remains expressed strongly through the medium of children's literature, and, in addition, texts produced in earlier times continue to be available to, and influence, child readers today. The stereotypes coalesce into three distinct types of behaviour, and these will be explored in Section 5.

5 Pedagogical, Baffled or Mad: Building Stereotypes

It has been demonstrated that the stereotypical academic is an old white male scientific professor working alone, with wild hair, likely to have a messy

---

[569] Reynolds and DeMoss, 'Super Higher Education: The Role of Academics in Comic Books', p. 1.

white beard, in a suit or lab coat: although these are often represented with humour and warmth, they echo the 'pale, male, and stale' establishment that manage our real-life public bodies.[570] Alongside these identifiable characteristics there are three key behavioural models that can be seen in this corpus: the professor as kindly teacher, the professor as baffled, blundering goon and the professor as dangerous, evil madman. Whilst the teacher is a positive but shallow depiction of academia, the ineffectual and evil stereotypes are pejorative about intellectual achievement, presenting a humorous but negative view of expertise and academia to a young audience. It is important to note, however, that these stereotypes provide a framework within which modern authors and illustrators can work, particularly in picture books. Playing with established constructs and constraints provides impetus to the plot, or an efficient vehicle to impart information. In this chapter the three behavioural stereotypes in the corpus will be surveyed, while also highlighting how they provide modern authors and illustrators with constraints around which narratives can successfully be built, often to encourage the child reader's own feelings of intellectual autonomy.

5.1 *The Stereotypical Professor as Teacher*

The first stereotype is that of a helpful, kindly teacher or intellectual guide. Academics appear as teachers to children throughout the corpus; to give but some examples: Professor Howard in the first book;[571] the teacher in *The Professor's Last Skate*, who regales his class with an adventure tale;[572] Professor Crow who advises the young woodland animals poorly but

---

[570] Flinders, Matthews and Eason, 'Are Public Bodies Still "Male, Pale and Stale"?'

[571] *The Parents' Best Gift: A New Spelling Book, Containing a Large Quantity of Reading, Spelling, etc. Professor Howard's First Step to Learning* (London: Ryle and Co., 1850).

[572] Oxley, 'The Professor's Last Skate'.

kindly;[573] Dr Cornelius, mentor and teacher to Prince Caspian;[574] Dr Monsoon Taggert, head of a finishing academy;[575] and Dr Chimp, classroom teacher in mortar board and gown in *Rupert the Bear*.[576] This pedagogical relationship provides a mechanism for children to come into contact with adult – or grandfather-like, given they are almost always male – experts, in a formalisation of the 'wise old man' Jungian trope, all the way through the corpus. In factual books it is a framing device, used as a personable way to explain science and industry to a childhood readership. For example, from its publication in 1950, Professor Brittain appeared every fortnight in the *Eagle* comic for at least the first few years of its publication, to explain scientific developments such as telescopes,[577] deep sea divers,[578] X-ray,[579] traffic lights[580] and motorcycle engines.[581] A kind, fatherly figure, it is also important to note that he explained science equally to both boys *and* girls, with characters called Bob and Joan asking him questions (although their relationship is never explained). For example,

---

[573] Cory, *Little Jack Rabbit and Professor Crow*. [574] Lewis, *Prince Caspian*.

[575] Matthews, *Dr Monsoon Taggert's Amazing Finishing Academy*.

[576] Redfern, *Rupert and the Rope Trick in Your Favourite Rupert Story Collection*, p. 26.

[577] Eagle, 'Professor Brittain Explains a Giant Telescope', 1(3), (London: Hulton Press, 28 April 1950a).

[578] Eagle, 'Professor Brittain Explains: Deep Sea Diving', 1(5), (London: Hulton Press, 12 May 1950c).

[579] Eagle, 'Professor Brittain Explains: X-Ray', 1(10), (London: Hulton Press, 16 June 1950d).

[580] Eagle, 'Professor Brittain Explains: Traffic Lights', 1(14), (London: Hulton Press, 14 July 1950e).

[581] Eagle, 'Professor Brittain Explains: Motor Cycle Engines', 1(18), (London: Hulton Press, 11 August 1950f).

Bob, Joan and the Professor at the Motor-cycle races.

[Joan asks] 'I'd like to know how a motor-bike works, Professor'.

[Professor Brittain replies] 'After this lap I'll try to explain the broad principles.'[582]

The Professor promotes science as a career for both genders: after explaining X-ray, Joan remarks, 'Yes, I'd love to be a radiographer!'[583]

We see this type of relationship throughout the corpus: the expert professorial father figure is used to explain facts, such as science and industry in the *So That's the Reason!* series,[584] maths in *Professor Googol's Flying Machine and Atomic Space Capsule Math Primer*,[585] biology in the Einstein-alike *Professor I. Q. Explores the Senses*,[586] the alphabet in *Learning Your Animal ABC's with Professor Hoot*[587] and physics in *Professor Astro Cat's Frontiers of Space*.[588] They are used, too, in official public health guidance: Professor Oonoose Q. Eckwoose explains food groups in a booklet made by the United States Department of Agriculture Office of Communication[589] and *Professor Bumblebee* provides a *Guide to Type 1 Diabetes* for Diabetes

[582] Ibid. Used with kind permission of the Dan Dare Corporation Limited.

[583] *Eagle*, 16 June 1950.

[584] R. R. Baker, *So That's the Reason!* (Chicago, IL: Reilly & Lee Co., 1939) onwards.

[585] S. W. Valenza Jr, *Professor Googols Flying Machine and Atomic Space Capsule Math Primer* (Self-published: Intergalactic Publishing Co., 1974).

[586] Simon and Kendrick, *Professor I. Q. Explores the Senses*.

[587] E. Ruble, *Learning Your Animal ABC's with Professor Hoot* (Guardian Angel Publishing, Inc., 2008).

[588] Walliman and Newman, *Professor Astro Cat's Frontiers of Space*.

[589] United States Department of Agriculture Office of Communication, *The Thing the Professor Forgot* (Pueblo, CO: US Department of Agriculture Consumer Information Center, 1975).

Australia.[590] These academics are nothing but kindly and helpful, and they can be used as role models; for example, in the cartoon *Oor Wullie*, the local policeman P.C. Murdoch remarks to Wullie, the child protagonist, 'Ye should be stickin' in tae yer lessons an' be brainy like the twa professors yonder – they ken a'thing!' (Figure 23)[591] However, there is little exploration of any individuality: the trope of the kindly pedagogue, used without need for explanation, sets up a well-known mechanism for framing explanation.

In fiction books, interactions with the teacher or mentor moves the plot forward, allowing them to learn more about the outside world, in tales based around science (often written by scientists). For example, the fictional Professor Hill explains the study of skunks (*The Professor and the Mysterious Box*[592]) and the tracking of whales (*The Professor and the Vanishing Flags*[593]) to children of a family he knows. Professor Potts' travels are a thinly veiled mechanism to teach children about the wildlife of Asia, North America[594] and Africa.[595] Professor

[590] E. Maritz and A. Maritz, *Professor Bumblebee's Guide to Type 1 Diabetes* (Glebe, New South Wales: Diabetes Australia, 2004).

[591] The Sunday Post, 'Oor Wullie'.

[592] R. G. Van Gelder, *The Professor and the Mysterious Box* (Irvington-on-Hudson, NY: Harvey House, 1964).

[593] R. G. Van Gelder, *The Professor and the Vanishing Flags* (Irvington-on-Hudson, NY: Harvey House, 1965). Richard George Van Gelder was the Curator of Mammalogy at the American Museum of Natural History in New York for twenty-five years – VIAF, 'Van Gelder, R. G.' (2016), https://viaf.org/viaf/1257462/ – bringing his expertise to these books.

[594] P. Spence and G. Chapman, *Professor Potts Meets the Animals in Asia* (London: Watts, 1981a); P. Spence, and G. Chapman, *Professor Potts Meets the Animals in North America* (London: Watts, 1981b).

[595] Wright and Chapman, *Professor Potts Meets the Animals in Africa*.

Figure 23 Oor Wullie, in The Sunday Post, 14 May 1944, p. 11. Note that the professors are holding books to indicate their expertise. Oor Wullie ® © DC Thomson & Co. Ltd 2017. Used By Kind Permission of DC Thomson & Co. Ltd. Image provided with thanks to The British Newspaper Archive (www.BritishNewspaperArchive.co.uk).

Inkling in the *Octonauts* original book series[596] is a fount of old-fashioned wisdom, patronal guidance and scientific explanation to his younger crew of adventurers (see Figure 8). The characters can sometimes be hollow and thinly drawn, but they are trustworthy sources of information both for other characters in the book and for readers. The (relatively recently) archetypical example of a fully fleshed out paternal figure is, of course, Professor Albus Dumbledore in the *Harry Potter* series,[597] who is wise old man, teacher, father figure and expert combined.

This sense of expertise and authority is turned on its head in various ways: recent creationist propaganda uses elderly male professors to demonstrate religious texts as fact: for example, *Professor Noah Thingertoo's Bible Fact Book*[598] and *Professor Bumblebrain's Bonkers Book on . . . God*.[599] For more comic effect, there are books that explain mythical beasts in the style of a natural history book: *Professor Dalrymple's Fairy Field Guide*;[600] Professor Miriam Carter in *The Mystery of Unicorns, The True History Revealed*.[601] In a humorous play on convention, professors can explain how the world works, but get it utterly wrong, such as in *Professor Mole's Machines (the amazing pop-up book of how things REALLY work!)* where a hamster on a wheel is shown to power a washing machine motor, and rabbits keep planes aloft by

---

[596] Meomi, *The Octonauts and the Only Lonely Monster* (San Francisco, CA: Immedium, 2006), onwards. The television series based on the Octonauts books followed in 2010.

[597] Rowling, *Harry Potter and the Philosopher's Stone* onwards.

[598] Gray, *Professor Noah Thingertoo's Bible Fact Book: Old Testament*.

[599] Robb, *Professor Bumblebrain's Bonkers Book on God*; see Figure 26.

[600] C. Engelbrecht, *Professor Dalrymple's Fairy Field Guide* (London: Running Press, 2007).

[601] Green, Hawkins, Williams, Andrew, Brown and Manson, *The Mystery of Unicorns*.

driving crankshafts: 'Faster, bunnies, faster!' 'We're tired, Daddy'.[602] Professor Gilderoy Lockhart, in *Harry Potter and the Chamber of Secrets*,[603] is a comically drawn cross between showman, ambitious big-head and bully, his public exposure as a fraud puncturing the sense of authority that comes with being a professor at Hogwarts.

The masters of this clash of pedagogical intention and erroneous information are Jeanne Willis and Tony Ross in their award-winning *Dr Xargle* picture books,[604] where the five-eyed, betentacled green alien in academic gown and mortar board prepares his class for an excursion to Earth. They each start in the same way: 'Good morning, class. Today we are going to learn about . . .'[605] and investigate various topics, where the explanation rapidly falls apart, revealing tension between both the truth that is known by the reader and the explanation given in the text, and the description of the scene and its accompanying illustration, in a multi-layered questioning and refocusing on habits, Western lifestyle and English language (Figure 24).

---

[602] J. O'Leary, *Professor Mole's Machines: The Amazing Pop-Up Book of How Things Really Work!* (London: Tango Books, 2004), p. 8. Used with kind permission of Tango Books.

[603] Rowling, *Harry Potter and the Chamber of Secrets*.

[604] Willis and Ross, *Dr Xargle's Book of Earthlets* onwards. There are seven books in total in the series. The third book, *Dr Xargle's Book of Earth Tiggers* (1990), won a highly commended runner-up award for the annual Kate Greenaway Medal, and was winner of the Sheffield Children's Book Award 1991: see J. Willis, 'Dr Xargle's Book of Earth Tiggers' (n. d.), http://jeannewillis.com/Book%20Pages/DrXEarthTiggers.html. A thirteen-episode television series based on the books was broadcast on British television in 1997: Big Cartoon Database, 'Earthlets (1997) Episode 1 – Dr Xargle Cartoon Episode Guide', (2016), www.bcdb.com/cartoon/71816-Earthlets.

[605] Used by kind permission of Andersen Press.

Figure 24 Dr Xargle explains cats gleefully but wrongly in Willis and Ross, *Dr Xargle's Book of Earth Tiggers* (p. 2). Used with kind permission of Andersen Press Ltd.

In the first book of the series, *Dr Xargle's Book of Earthlets* (1988), babies: 'come in many colours . . . but not green. They have one head and only two eyes, two short tentacles with pheelers on the end, and two long tentacles called leggies'.[606] The baby is shown being tickled by Dr Xargle's tentacles, questioning the assumed normality of the human body. 'They have square claws which they use to frighten off wild beasts known as Tibbles and Marmaduke'.[607] The baby is shown happily and firmly pulling the tails of two cats, who are desperately trying to get away, evidently terrorised by the baby, who has overturned their water bowl, leaving a dummy as a calling card in their food, allowing the reader to revel in the clash of picture and explanation. After a series of explanations, Dr Xargle comments, 'That is the end of today's lesson. If you are all very good and quiet we are going to put our disguises on and visit Earth to see some real Earthlets. The space ship leaves in five minutes . . .'[608] In later books in the series, these misunderstandings anticipate that visits will go wrong in the closing illustration of the book: in *Dr Xargle's Book of Earth Mobiles* (1991), Matron arranges for the students to go on a train ride, which turns out to be a fairground ghost train; in *Dr Xargle's Book of Earth Weather* (1992), the aliens end up dressed as miniature Santas singing 'Hark the horrid angels sing'[609] at a summer garden party to the bemusement of the humans; in *Dr Xargle's Book of Earth Tiggers* (1992) they end up in close proximity to a tiger by mistake. This play with the role of the teacher, known facts, conflicting illustration and retooled language, revels in tensions and differences, lampooning expertise and allowing the child reader to be the expert of their own lifestyle, knowing more than the

---

[606] Willis and Ross, *Dr Xargle's Book of Earthlets*, pp. 3–4. [607] Ibid., p. 5.
[608] Ibid., pp. 26–28. [609] Willis and Ross, *Dr Xargle's Book of Earth Weather*, p. 32.

Was handing them a cup of tea each

Figure 25 Professor Branestawm and The Colonel, being served tea by Mrs Flittersnoop after they blow up the Palace of Squiglatania. In Hunter, *The Incredible Adventures of Professor Branestawm*, p. 21, illustrated by W. Heath Robinson. Public Domain.

alien professor or his visiting hordes of aliens will ever do.[610] This clever and funny series, which has been recommended in the teaching of science in

---

[610] These are my son Edward's favourite, precisely 'because he gets it all wrong, Mummy!'

schools,[611] would also not function had professorial tropes in children's literature not previously been established.

5.2 *The Stereotypical Muddle-Head*

In a recurrent motif throughout the corpus, professors are routinely baffled, eccentric and ineffectual, with no grasp on the real world. The inventions and science often fail, accompanied by slapstick humour, and they demonstrate very poor life skills. A Professor in *The Forgetful Forget-me-not*[612] asks the flower why it is so named, and is curtly told to go away and use his skill and look it up in books himself, the plant having forgotten too. In *Sylvie and Bruno*, 'The Professor' is

> a wonderfully clever man, you know. Sometimes he says things
> that only the Other Professor can understand. Sometimes he
> says things that nobody can understand![613]

Little Jack Rabbit regularly comments on how the world works, pointing out that his friend 'Professor Crow didn't tell me that', in a failure of the professor's *Little Book of Wisdom*.[614]

The archetypal absent-minded professor who creates malfunctioning inventions is, of course, *Professor Branestawm* (appearing in thirteen books from 1933):

---

[611] K. Ansberry and E. R. Morgan, *Picture-Perfect Science Lessons: Using Children's Books to Guide Inquiry* (Arlington, VA: National Science Teachers Association Press, 2010).

[612] O. Herford, 'The Forgetful Forgetmenot', *St Nicholas*, XX(10) (New York, NY: Scribner's, 1893), p. 775.

[613] Carroll, *Sylvie and Bruno*, p. 13.

[614] Cory, *Little Jack Rabbit and Professor Crow*, p. 9.

> [A]lthough the Professor was so clever, or perhaps because he
> was so clever, he was absent-minded. He was so busy thinking of
> wonderful things like new diseases or new moons that he simply
> hadn't time to think of ordinary things like old spectacles.[615]

These books also establish the role of the Professor's housekeeper, Mrs
Flittersnoop, as an essential enabler as well as foil (Figure 25).

The publishing success of Branestawm colours the characteristics of
the academics that follow in children's literature. The Professor in *Mistress
Masham's Repose*

> was a failure, but he did his best to hide it. One of his failings
> was that he could scarcely write, except in a twelfth century
> hand, in Latin, with abbreviations. Another was that, although
> his cottage was crammed with books, he seldom had anything to
> eat. He could not tell from Adam . . . what the latest quotation
> of Imperial Chemicals was upon the Stock Exchange.[616]

These baffled professors are often illustrated with humour, linking concentra-
tion and intellectual obsession with the reason they are incapable in other
aspects of life. Webb's illustration affectionately lampoons and characterises
the features of hard-thinking professors, summing up the common stereotype
in one handy graphic in Figure 26

The confusion and baffled nature of the academics, who are supposed to
be in control, is a plot device which causes juxtapositions to move the story
along. Professor Magnus MacWhizzer invents a time machine but cannot drive
it:

---

[615] Hunter, *The Incredible Adventures of Professor Branestawm*, p. 1.

[616] White, *Mistress Masham's Repose*, p. 17.

Figure 26 Professor Ponsonby in Parker, *Professor Ponsonby, McIntosh and the Wool Bug* (p. 39), illustrated by Philip Webb. Used with permission of the illustrator and rights owner, Philip Webb.

I must say I'm getting rather good at working this vehicle . . . We shall arrive several degrees north or south of the solar system . . . It will be yesterday, next week, or the year two thousand and one. That is the finest degree of accuracy with which I can predict our

> course. If you want greater precision then I must recommend that
> next time you ride in a Number 12 bus.[617]

The erratic, chaotic travels allow the professor, along with his housekeeper
and his great-great-niece and -nephew, to travel through space, although the
professor himself is ultimately stranded by his invention when 'lost in a
delicious daydream, the Professor overbalanced, tripped over his own toe,
and one flailing arm caught the lever marked GO . . .':[618] he is shown
disappearing in the pop of a bubble. Likewise, the gap between what the
professor perceives and what the action is drives forward the picture book
Cockatoos,[619] where the eccentric and absent-minded Professor Dupont is
repeatedly outsmarted by his pet birds, who hide all over his house (providing
a counting game to the reader). Professor Quickly doesn't notice – unlike
everyone else, including the reader, who can see a ghost at the window – that
his new house is haunted.[620] Professor Yahoo is tasked by the Queen to
collect a menagerie so she can have a zoo of her own, but trips over a goat
and breaks his glasses, leading him to collect a random selection of things
mistaken for exotic animals:

> It was one crazy mix-up right after another –
> They captured a pickle and somebody's mother!
> They captured a mailbox, a swing set, some spoons.
> They snared a T. V. that was showing cartoons.
> And he didn't stop there, that silly Yahoo –

---

[617] Englander, *The Amazing Professor and his Travels in Time*, p. 18. [618] Ibid., p. 27.
[619] Blake, *Cockatoos*. [620] Harris and Hingley, *Professor Quickly*.

He made them catch kites!
What a weird thing to do![621]

 The denouement, in this case, is that the Queen – who has broken her glasses too – is delighted by the collection, but mistakes Professor Yahoo for a talking goose, and so he now lives happily in a zoo enclosure (Figure 27).

 Professors get nicknames because of their baffled nature:

> Sometimes I think that Professor Albert lived millions of years ago, too. He is very absent-minded. One day, when Professsor Albert was wearing his shirt inside out for the third day in a row, Sipo said 'I think there is coconut milk in his head, instead of a brain.' After that, we called him Professor Coconut.[622]

Professors change their own names, too:

> When he said goodbye, Professor Llawonk confided to Jack Dawe that his real name was Professor Knowall but he has changed it round because he really did not know very much.[623]

Comment is made about the uselessness of the inventions and science undertaken. The reader in *Did I Ever Tell You How Lucky You Are?*[624] is asked to

[621] N. Evans, *The Mixed-Up Zoo of Professor Yahoo* (Kansas City, MO: Junior League of Kansas City, 1993), pp. 16–17. Reproduced by permission of the Junior League of Kansas City, Missouri, from *The Mixed-Up Zoo of Professor Yahoo*, written and illustrated by Nate Evans. All rights reserved.

[622] Gelman and Richter, *Professor Coconut and the Thief*, p. 15; see Figure 11.

[623] Uncle B and Green, *Jack Dawe Super Scientist and the Professors*, p. 19.

[624] Dr Seuss, *Did I Ever Tell You How Lucky You Are?* (New York, NY: Random House, 1973), p. 28.

"I did a great job!" cried Professor Yahoo.

Figure 27 Professor Yahoo congratulates himself for collecting a 'Polar Bear and Penguin' for his zoo. Reproduced by permission of the Junior League of Kansas City, Missouri, from Evans, *The Mixed-Up Zoo of Professor Yahoo* (p. 20).

consider how much more fortunate they are than Professor de Breeze, who has spent three decades trying to teach Irish ducks to read the Jivanese language. The ducks are pictured being lectured, and are unconvinced. Likewise, Professor Ponsonby (Figure 26)

> was always inventing things to help ... There was no statue to Professor Ponsonby in Baaville ... That was because so far none of professor's inventions had worked. But he still invented non-stop, usually when the rest of Baaville was fast asleep in bed.[625]

The engineer Professor Von Bean in *Silly Stories* spends his lifetime inventing a machine:

> 'I know I'm persistent!' cried Von Bean's young assistant
> 'And I love your machine through and through!
> The lights flash on top when it spins it can't stop!
> But tell me – what on earth does it DO?'
> With a terribly cry and a long drawn-out sigh
> Von Bean said, 'Oh what a fool!
> I never once thought – I've really been caught
> This machine does *nothing useful at all!*'[626]

[625] J. Parker, *Professor Ponsonby, McIntosh and the Wool Bug* (Auckland, New Zealand: Harper Collins, 1994), pp. 10–11. Used by kind permission of John Parker.

[626] A. Charman and D. Catchpole, *Silly Stories* (Bath: Parragon Books, 2001), p. 236. The same story, but retold in non-rhyming fashion, appears in C. F. Alexander, T. Barrett, A. J. Brown et al., *A Story a Day, 365 Stories and Rhymes for Boys* (Bath: Parragon, 2008): 'While Professor Von Bean was getting more and more excited, his assistant looked very worried.

'"But what does it do?" he asked timidly.

'The professor scratched his head and thought.

Whatever they are doing – whether inventing, undertaking scientific experiments or digging on an archaeological site – many of the academics are shown as endearingly ineffectual and pointless, in a deprecatory (and at times vituperative) depiction of the 'life of the mind'.

Lectures and classes are depicted as confusing and boring. The Professor's lecture in *Sylvie and Bruno Concluded* (Figure 7),[627] despite featuring miniaturised elephants, and explosions, is rambling, has no topic and loses the audience's attention. '"How long must we wait?" grumbled the Emperor.'[628] Professor Mudweed in the *Boffin Boy* series comments, 'None of you are clever enough to understand my invention, but I'll try and explain it . . .', at which point, an audience member thinks, 'This is going to be really boring',[629] in an exaggeration of the stereotype of a yawn-inducing academic lecture.[630] Professor Bumblebrain comments, 'I do hope you are finding my lecture of interest. When you have a brain as large as mine, it is so very easy to bore an audience to death' (Figure 28).[631] Science, in particular, is portrayed as a magical source only accessible to academics, linking to stage-tricks and conjuring, but also crossing into fantastical thinking, showing intellect as sitting between realism and impossibility, building on tropes of nonsense-writing,

'"Oh dear, oh dear!" he sighed. "What a fool I have been! Why didn't I think of that? It does absolutely nothing useful at all!"' (p. 17). Both used by kind permission of Parragon books.

[627] Carroll, *Sylvie and Bruno Concluded*.

[628] Carroll, *Sylvie and Bruno Concluded*, p. 343.

[629] Orme and Richardson, *Boffin Boy and the Wizard of Edo*, p. 1; see Figure 6. Used by kind permission of David Orme.

[630] D. Orme, Personal communication: 'Professor Mudweed', reply to email from Melissa Terras, 9 February 2017.

[631] Robb, *Professor Bumblebrain's Bonkers Book on God*, p. 47. Used by kind permission of CWR.

Figure 28 Robb, *Professor Bumblebrain's Bonkers Book on God* (p. 53). Used with permission, CWR. Notice, also, the Einstein-like Bumblebrain.

of grotesques and of caricature.[632] The bafflement in these cases creates a gap between the intellectual authority of the professor and the knowledge of the child reader, who can see, via illustrations, where the adults are ineffectual, wrong and boring, and not in control of the environments around them. The childhood audience is encouraged to explore the gaps, in an intellectual equivalent of spotting that the emperor has no clothes.

The apparent confusion at real life is often stressed by the juxtaposition of normal and magical thinking: Professor Bull

> was fond of three things: music … radishes … and his umbrella, Philip … 'My goodness gracious!' said the professor. 'Hardly a radish left in the house! Philip, we must see to that at once.' And he took up Philip and his market basket.[633]

Eccentric, baffled professors are, then, playing with logic and rationalisation in an extension to and in the tradition of nineteenth-century nonsense writing, where fantastic adventures are playfully framed against known, mundane reality in a 'perfect tension between meaning and absence of meaning'[634] that is amusing (particularly to a childhood audience) and that encourages the reader to think about normal behaviour and what it is to be an adult. These professors act, rather like Mary Poppins, as 'the conduit between reality and fantasy, the structural interface in the text',[635] allowing safe exploration of the

---

[632] R. McGillis, 'Humour and the body in children's literature', in M. O. Grenby and A. Immel (eds.), *Cambridge Companion to Children's Literature* (Cambridge: Cambridge University Press, 2009), pp. 258–271, p. 265.

[633] W. Lipkind and G. Schreiber, *Professor Bull's Umbrella* (New York, NY: Children's Literary Guild and Viking, 1954), p. 1.

[634] W. Tigges, *An Anatomy of Literary Nonsense* (Amsterdam: Rodopi, 1998), p. 4.

[635] J. Webb, 'Connecting with Mary Poppins', in D. C. Thacker, and J. Webb, *Introducing Children's Literature: From Romanticism to Postmodernism* (New York, NY: Routledge, 2002), pp. 114–121, p. 115.

impossible and illogical where 'the structure of the text enables readers to suggest their own conclusions because there is a pattern of connection which moves from the known to the unknown'[636] provided by 'a real figure of authority and didacticism ... and the fantastic facilitator of magical experiences'.[637] While professors are shown in pejorative fashion as being ineffectual, and their work meaningless, which (as we shall see) plays into the view of the scientist in popular culture and actively reinforces distrust of expertise, this mechanism can also be more complex: giving authors and illustrators a place to play with known constraints, using tropes to explore authority and intellect via nonsense.

The mostly ineffectual nature of these academics is reflected in their challenging names. Pedagogues are apparent, with three Professor Wisemans,[638] two Professor IQs[639] and a Professor Boffin,[640] Professor Egghead,[641] Professor Inkling,[642] Professor Noodle[643] and Professor Tidymind.[644] However, there are far more with pejorative names. There are

[636] Ibid. [637] Ibid., p. 117.

[638] M. Rey and H. A. Rey, 'Curious George gets a medal' (1957), in M. Rey and H. A. Rey, *The Complete Adventures of Curious George* (Boston, MA: Houghton Mifflin Harcourt, 2001); Rey and Rey, *Curious George's Dinosaur Discovery*; Rey and Rey, *Curious George and the Dinosaur*.

[639] Simon and Kendrick, *Professor I. Q. Explores the Senses*; Qinsheng, *IQ Maths Professor: In the Case of the Time Machine* (Singapore: Henry Marketing Services, 2003).

[640] Alexander, *Professor Boffin's Umbrella*.

[641] R. Wyler and J. Robinson, *Professor Egghead's Best Riddles* (New York, NY: Simon and Schuster, 1973).

[642] Meomi *The Octonauts and the Only Lonely Monster* (San Francisco: Immedium 2006)

[643] C. Vurnakes and K. Dunne, *Professor Noodle's Circus School* (New York, NY: Playmore, 1992).

[644] Australian Government Publishing Service, *Professor Crackinbottle and Professor Tidymind*.

two Professor Bumbles,[645] a Professor Blabbermouth,[646] Professor Bumblebrain,[647] Professor Bumphead,[648] Professor Clickilty Klunk,[649] Professor Dinglebat,[650] Professor Doodle,[651] Professor Dribble,[652] Professor Hogwash,[653] Professor Von Hardbum,[654] Professor Muddlehead,[655] Professor P. Brain,[656] Professor PigglePoggle,[657] Professor Pingwit,[658] Professor Poopypants,[659] Professor Poppoff,[660] Professor Stupido[661] and Professor

[645] H. Amery and C. King, *The Knowhow Book of Experiments* (London: Usborne, 1977); D. Napp and H. Schmitt-Thomas, *Professor Bumble and the Monster of the Deep* (New York, NY: Abrams Books for Young Readers, 2008).

[646] Watts, *Professor Blabbermouth on the Moon*.

[647] Robb, *Professor Bumblebrain's Bonkers Book on God*.

[648] Johns, *The Fairies' Annual*.

[649] C. Klunk and T. Lynch, *A Puppy Named Rufus* (Clearwater, BC: Down the Path Pub., 2009).

[650] Noonan, *Professor Dinglebat and the Dynamic Dog De-Barker*.

[651] C. MacIntosh and S. Sack, *Professor Doodle's Upside Down Sideways Puzzle Book* (Orlando, FL: Tribune Pub., 1992).

[652] Kettle, *Professor Dribble*.

[653] K. M. Crawford, *Professor Horton Hogwash's Museum of Ridiculous. A Hysterical Drawing Folly* (Happily Ever Art Publishing, 2011).

[654] A. MacDonald and N. Baines, *The Revenge of the Green Meanie* (London: Bloomsbury, 2014).

[655] IPC Magazines, 'Toby and Professor Muddlehead', *Toby and Seesaw* 95 (London: IPC Magazines Ltd, 19 November 1977).

[656] McLeay, *Professor P. Brain's Astronomical Trip*.

[657] Charlton and Matheson, *Professor Pigglepoggle*.

[658] B. Crump and L. Kriegler, *Professor Pingwit and the Pungapeople* (Auckland, New Zealand: Hachette NZ, 2009).

[659] Pilkey, *Captain Underpants and the Perilous Plot of Professor Poopypants*

[660] B. Willsher, *Tales of Professor Popoff* (London: Peal Press, 1966).

[661] A. Griffiths, *39-Story Treehouse* (Sydney: Pan MacMillan Australia, 2013).

Whatzit.[662] Those who are given 'real' names have ones that are foreign, unusual or difficult to the English tongue, highlighting their otherness; for example: Professor Euclid Bullfinch;[663] Professor Pompilius McGrath;[664] Professor Mickimecki;[665] and Professor Aristides Pilaster.[666]

There are also three Professor Potts[667] and a Professor Pots,[668] Professor Nutter,[669] Professor Nut,[670] Professor Coconut[671] and Professor Crackinbottle,[672] pointing to another theme in the corpus: madness.

5.3 The Stereotypical Madman

There is little thought given to the impact of ableist language by authors: 'Sometimes I think my friend Professor Solomon Snickerdoodle is a little funny in the head.'[673] Books even have madness in the title, such as or *My*

---

[662] D. Brown and B. Crook, *Professor Whatzit and Carmine the Cat* (Los Angeles, CA: Tom Thumb Music, 1989).

[663] Williams and Abrashkin, *Danny Dunn and the Anti-Gravity Paint*.

[664] O. de Mejo, *The Professor of Etiquette: A Guide to the Do's and Don'ts of Civilised Living* (New York, NY: Philomel Books, 1992).

[665] Wahl, *SOS Bobmobile*. [666] Timmermans, *The Great Balloon Race*.

[667] Wright and Chapman, *Professor Potts Meets the Animals in Africa*; Roxbee Cox and Atkinson, *Whatever Happened to Professor Potts?*; Potts 2006.

[668] S. Pitts, S. Durrant and D. St Pierre, *Professor Pots Presents the Fantastical Flight of the Ugglebuck Bird* (Chelmsford: J's Hospice, 2009).

[669] Webb, *Professor Nutter and the Curse of the Pharaoh's Tomb*.

[670] Blackwood and Skilton, *Doctor Crotchet's Symphony*.

[671] Gelman and Richter, *Professor Coconut and the Thief*.

[672] Australian Government Publishing Service, *Professor Crackinbottle and Professor Tidymind*.

[673] P. Murray and P. Dann, *Professor Solomon Snickerdoodle's Air Science Tricks* (Plymouth, MN: Child's World, 1998), p. 1, © The Child's World, www.childs world.com. Used by kind permission.

Father the Mad Professor,[674] *Mad Professor: Concoct Extremely Weird Science Projects,*[675] *Dr Brad Has Gone Mad*[676] and *The Mad Professor's Workshop.*[677]

The apparent madness of academics is closely associated with genius:

> Professor Blabbermouth was as bright as buttons. There was no doubt about it. She had enough university degrees to paper her toilet walls. Some people said she was a genius. Some people said she was a nutter. It was all a matter of opinion . . . All those brains and nothing to use them on made her do rather . . . eccentric things. Like cycling backwards to the shop in the belief it saved time. Or for a complete week never using the letter 'e' whn spaking to popl. She never explained her reasons for this. And nobody thought to ask.[678]

The dishevelled, big-haired appearances of the academics feed into this slap-stick, oddball otherworldliness, where the madness can be kindly and eccentric, separated from (and not understanding) cultural norms. Doctor Crotchet and Professor Nut devote their energies to recording a symphony that is so loud and awful it terrorises their town, without them noticing.[679] Professor Peekaboo is asked, 'would you subscribe to the view that you're essentially

---

[674] Odgers and Nye, *My Father the Mad Professor*.

[675] Frauenfelder, *Mad Professor: Concoct Extremely Weird Science Projects*.

[676] D. Gutman, *Dr Brad has Gone Mad!* (New York, NY: Harper Collins Children's Books, 2009).

[677] J. Matthews and C. Matthews, *The Mad Professor's Workshop* (Dorking: Templar Publishing, 2010).

[678] Watts, *Professor Blabbermouth on the Moon*, pp. 1–8.

[679] Blackwood and Skilton, *Doctor Crotchet's Symphony*.

eccentric?' – and agrees.[680] Professor Molecule's friends often laugh and shake their heads at him, commenting, 'What a crazy Professor!'[681] Professor Oliver Query is suddenly custodian to his teenage daughter in *My Father The Mad Professor*,[682] and his eccentricities, and the differences between his own lifestyle and that of 'normal' Americans, provides the mechanism for the teenage narrator to explore father–daughter relationships and bonding with a parent, post-divorce:

> I have been living with my father now for nearly a year. He still eats Estonian eggplant with that deep-sea, iodine-rich plankton, but Quintus [the parrot] has sunflower seeds and I eat baked beans. It's not a perfect life. My father still blows up if I meddle with his experiments. I still blow up if he meddles with my clothes or food. And things are decidedly weird. The other day, a meteorite landed in the chimney. . .[683]

However, alongside the eccentricities and questionable mental health comments, comes representation of ever-present malice and Machiavellianism:

> it looked as if all of the Earth's dilemmas would be fixed for ever. But who would have believed that in just a few short weeks, Professor Poopypants would be trying to take over the planet in a fit of frenzied rage?[684]

[680] Agard and Kitamura, *Points of View with Professor Peekaboo*, p. 4.

[681] Wyatt, *Professor Molecule's Fantastic Listening Machine*, p. 35.

[682] Odgers and Nye, *My Father the Mad Professor*. [683] Ibid., p. 59.

[684] Pilkey, *Captain Underpants and the Perilous Plot of Professor Poopypants*, p. 24.

The evil scientific desire for dominance and destruction is revealed in numerous texts, where the madness often comes to define them. Doctor Daffney in the *Boffin Boy* series is a 'famous mad scientist, you know.'[685] 'Mad Professor Erasmus' in *Stitch Head, The Ghost of Grotteskew* is 'considered by most to be the maddest professor of all. He had spent a lifetime creating crazy creations.'[686] Doctors are more likely to be evil than professors: so much so that the villain in *Professor Blabbermouth on the Moon*,[687] 'The meanest and most jealous scientist in the world, and a man who smelt of aftershave,'[688] is simply known as Doctor Doctor: 'He had been plotting and being evil all day, and Doctor Doctor was tired.'[689] The threats posed by these characters are usually told with humour, and the violence is often entertaining, such as the glorious Dr Frankenstinker, who exercises his madness as if he were the naughtiest boy in the school (Figure 29).

Dr Frankenstinker – his name a comic play on Frankenstein just rude enough to be funny for an infant school audience[690] – plays with the mad scientist idea, with his evil ways reflecting the kind of things children would be told off for, converted to science fiction. The author, Timothy Knapman, commented:

[685] D. Orme and P. Richardson, *Boffin Boy and the Poison Garden* (Winchester: Ransom Publishing, 2013), p. 2. Used by kind permission of David Orme.

[686] G. Bass and P. Williamson, *Stitch Head* (London: Stripes Pub., 2012), p. 16.

[687] Watts, *Professor Blabbermouth on the Moon*. [688] Ibid., p. 18. [689] Ibid., p. 23.

[690] 'He was originally called Dr Cosmo Zang. The name Frankenstinker occurred to me (as far too many things do) while staring out of a train window. I was visiting a school in Hemel Hempstead with the first Mungo book and I tried out the story of the second – which was then called *Mungo and the Clockwork Spiders From Space* – with the children there. When I got to the villain's entrance, I gave them the choice of names. They laughed at the name Frankenstinker and not at Zang, so Frankenstinker he became,' T. Knapman, Personal communication: 'Quick Question about Dr Frankenstinker in Mungo and the Spiders from Space', reply to email from Melissa Terras, 3 February 2017.

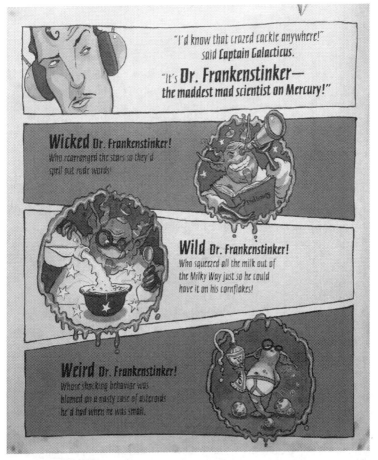

Figure 29 From MUNGO AND THE SPIDERS FROM SPACE by Timothy Knapman, illustrated by Adam Stower, p. 9. Text copyright © 2007 by Timothy Knapman. Illustrations copyright © 2007 by Adam Stower. Used by permission of Dial Books for Young Readers, an imprint of Penguin Young Readers Group, a division of Penguin Random House LLC. Notice that, despite his naughtiness, Dr Frankenstinker consults a dictionary.

there's often no room in a picture book to create a fully-functioning world of the author's own (like the one that, say, J. K. Rowling has furnished for her readers) so you sometimes take character types and settings 'off the peg', as it were, and play variations on them.[691]

In *Mungo and the Spiders From Space*, the evil scientist needs no introduction, being accepted by the reader as a fully formed troublemaker and nemesis without the need for backstory, eventually thwarted by child hero Mungo, in a text that plays with conventions (the books are 'deliberatively [given] a retro look ... the Dan Dare-style comic of Spiders'[692]).

In the case of Dr Frankenstinker, Knapman reflected back to his childhood viewing:

> I loved science fiction and horror as a child and I remember evil mad scientists from those days – Frankenstein himself most of all (I remember being very excited when the BBC showed a season of the original, black and white Universal horror movies). Though I have to say that the mad scientists that meant something to me back then were kindly ones – Doctor Who, in his manic Tom Baker incarnation, and Professor Branestawm. I used a mad scientist villain in *Spiders From Space* for the same reason that I'd chosen a pirate book for Mungo to be reading in [*Mungo and the*] *Picture Book Pirates*.[693] There hadn't been any mad

---

[691] Knapman, personal communication, February 2017. [692] Ibid.

[693] T. Knapman, *Mungo and the Picture Book Pirates* (2006).

scientists in popular culture for a while, just as there hadn't been any pirates, so I thought it was time to revisit the idea.[694]

Dr Frankenstinker sits within a long tradition of evil scientists, played up for comic effect, in an intertextual rollicking space adventure that nods to the film, television, and texts that have come before it, expecting the reader to be aware of the conventions used. The humour here is in a long tradition of classic picture books reminding us that

> children expand their worlds through misbehaviour – and how mischief can be a surprisingly constructive, and even creative, means by which children adapt to, and seek to revise, societal and familial boundaries.[695]

Fully illustrated picture books for three- to five-year-olds contain many straightforward stereotypical academic madmen who are introduced without the need for explanation, such is their known trope. In *Traction Man Is Here*,[696] Evil Doctor Sock tries to force a cupcake to be his bride, and wicked Professor Spade keeps dollies captive (Figure 30). This references, and plays with the casual misogyny and gender structure of, boys' own adventure tales:[697] the sock and spade in *Traction Man Is Here* are actors playing the part of the typical baddie, sprung from the boyish imagination of Traction Man's owner, who drives the plot on. However, these stereotypical structures are subverted: both

[694] Knapman, personal communication, February 2017

[695] E. H. Spitz, *Inside Picture Books* (New Haven, CT: Yale University Press, 1999), p. 162.

[696] Grey, *Traction Man is Here*.

[697] C. Marquis, 'Romancing the home: gender, empire and the South Pacific', in B. L. Clark and M. R. Higonnet (eds.), *Girls, Boys, Books, Toys: Gender in Children's Literature and Culture* (JHU Press, 2000), pp. 53–68, p. 62.

Figure 30 Traction Man sets out to rescue Cupcake, but is thwarted by his ridiculous knitted romper suit. Artwork: *Mini Grey*, from *Traction Man Is Here*, by *Mini Grey*, Published by *Jonathan Cape*, Reprinted by permission of The Random House Group Limited. © 2005.[698]

[698] Grey, *Traction Man is Here*, p. 21.

Doctor Sock and the harassed cupcake forget about the villain and victim roles when confronted with Traction Man's ridiculous green knitted outfit, which has been provided lovingly by the boy's grandmother, and worn by Traction Man unwillingly: everyone laughs, and the structures and predicted plot line disintegrate.

Similarly, the denouement of *The Astonishing Secret of Awesome Man*[699] is that Awesome Man is the alter ego of a boy, who imagines foes for his superhero character that short-cut straight to established stereotypes in superhero set pieces. Awesome Man takes on Professor Von Evil, who is illustrated inside a marauding, egg-shaped metallic robot with a pointed top and robot legs, that is shooting out green goo from its arms. The professor is shown through a green-tinted window in the centre, that reveals a small old bespectacled man in lab coat with long, pointed, Einstein-like hair and a maniacal expression as he pulls leavers, controlling the bot (Figure 31). Here is the entire mention of the evil professor, from entrance to vanquishing, in the picture book:

> Here comes Professor Von Evil in his Antimatter Slimebot! Antimatter slime is extra gross![700]
>
> But okay, check this out. I change into my secret identity – and the dude just sklooshes right past me. Do you see me? Professor Von Evil doesn't![701]

---

[699] Chabon and Parker, *The Astonishing Secret of Awesome Man*. [700] Ibid., p. 11.
[701] Ibid., p. 12.

Figure 31 Professor Von Evil from Chabon and Parker, *The Astonishing Secret of Awesome Man* (p. 11). Used with permission, HarperCollins Children's Books.

Then I just sneak up behind him, slap a big old power grip on his pointy head . . . and SKA-RUNCH! 'It[']s time the professor learned his lesson!'[702]

Awesome Man then moves swiftly on to his next adventure, fighting his 'arch nemesis',[703] The Flaming Eyeball. This playing with established stereotypes of adventure and superhero stories, in the abbreviation of children's play, highlights how entrenched doctors and professors are as comic villains in later children's literature, with no prior knowledge needed about the character or role to set up the scene, in a postmodern borrowing and playing with established frameworks, structures and histories. Of course the professor is an evil version of Einstein with a marauding robot that will attack the city with science! *Of course!* The story is not focussed on the Professor, but is about the growing autonomy, and imagination, of the child, who plays with established stereotypes.

These evil representations of intelligence become more threatening as the predicted audience for the texts advances. Dr Morrison (the first of three evil woman), in the *Jinty* story *Battle of the Wills* (1977), wants to demonstrate how she can clone teenage girls, despite the effect on them, for scientific glory. Doctor Daffney wants to turn everyone into bonsai trees[704] in a reference to the Daphne and Apollo myth (Figure 32).[705] Professor Dolores Umbridge, in *Harry Potter and the Order of the Phoenix* (2003), is malevolent, and abuses both her power and the children and adults in her care.

In a 2018 study, 'male villains were eight times more likely to appear compared to female villains' in children's books:[706] wickedness is heavily

---

[702] Ibid., p. 13. Used by kind permission of HarperCollins Children's Books.

[703] Ibid., p. 14. [704] Orme and Richardson, *Boffin Boy and the Poison Garden*.

[705] Orme, personal communication, February 2017.

[706] Ferguson, 'Must monsters always be male?'

Figure 32 Boffin Boy and his friend Polly held captive by Doctor Daphne, in Orme and Richardson, *Boffin Boy and the Poison Garden* (p. 19). Used by kind permission of David Orme and Peter Richardson.

gendered, and the majority of evil professors here are male. Dedrick the Professor invents a Robobeast army that will take control of nature and the oceans.[707] Professor Aldous P. Lickpenny, criminal mastermind, wants to turn children into his robot 'mechanizmos".[708] Professor Severus Snape is a complex, vindictive, often intimidating, *presumed* evil figure in the *Harry Potter* series.[709] Lord Asriel is a dominating, stern and calculatingly cruel presence in the *His Dark Materials* trilogy (although in the end shows his love for his child and former lover).[710] Professor Gargoyle, in a school story for older children which revolves around sinister teachers, mutant two-headed rodents and tentacles that threaten to overpower unsuspecting pupils, is shown dislocating his shark-toothed jaw, snake style, and holding up a rat to eat it whole in a frightening illustration in *Professor Gargoyle, Tales from Lovecraft Middle School*, showing that professors' evil madness can also be terrifying.[711] Likewise, children are lured home with the 'Mad Professor's Daughter' with gruesome consequences in the Allan Ahlberg poem:

> A whole class, like sheep we were
> Like lambs to the slaughter,
> . . . Don't leave us to the father of
> The Mad Professor's Daughter![712]

This piece is commonly placed on reading lists for children aged seven to ten, and regularly recommended for a poetry exercise in UK primary

---

[707] Blade, *Sea Quest* series onwards.

[708] M. Jocelyn, R. Scrimger, T. Walker and C. Dávila, *Viminy Crowe's Comic Book* (Toronto: Tundra Books, 2014).

[709] Rowling, *Harry Potter and the Philosopher's Stone* onwards.

[710] Pullman, *Northern Lights* onwards.

[711] C. Gilman and E. Smith, *Professor Gargoyle* (Philadelphia, PA: Quirk Books, 2012).

[712] Ahlberg, 'The Mad Professor's Daughter' in *Heard It in the Playground*, pp. 70–71. Used by kind permission of Puffin Books.

schools.[713] A tale of being lured away from the safe school setting into the hands of the Mad Professor is enjoyable when the readers are safe enough to explore fear,[714] in a reminder that 'much humour for children is exaggerated, fantasy writ large, a reminder of the monstrous and the freakish'.[715] Children know that when academics are not telling them how the world works, or being ineffectual, boring and eccentric, they are being destructive and evil: readers can enjoy the thrill, laugh at the difference and explore the threat safely from tales in books. Nevertheless, the mad, evil stereotype is reinforced: intellect is predictably other, strange and dangerous. The irony here, of course, is that there are increasing levels of stress, anxiety and mental illness being reported by those working within the University system, due in part to the increasing pressures being placed on those operating within the academic machine.[716]

---

[713] For example, see G. Booth, *Practice Papers English: Age 9–10. Assess Your Child's Key Stage 2 Progress* (London: Letts Educational, 1999), p. 46; Bedford Borough Council, 'Poems for Ages 5–9', The Virtual Library, Central Bedfordshire Library Services (2015), http://virtual-library.culturalservices.net/webingres/bedford shire/vlib/0.children_teenagers/booklist_poems_5to9.htm; Primary Resources, 'English: Text Level Fiction: Poetry' (2016), www.primaryresources.co.uk/eng lish/englishC7f.htm.

[714] M. Wilson, 'Teenage tales', *Children's Literature in Education*, 28(3), (1997), pp. 151–162.

[715] McGillis, 'Humour and the body in children's literature', p. 267.

[716] W. H. Gmelch, P. K. Wilke and N. P. Lovrich, 'Dimensions of stress among university faculty: factor-analytic results from a national study', *Research in Higher Education*, 24, (1986), 266–286; J. K. Dua, 'Job stressors and their effects on physical health, emotional health, and job satisfaction in a university', *Journal of Educational Administration*, 32, (1994), 59–78; G. Kinman, 'Pressure points: a review of research on stressors and strains in UK academics', *Educational Psychology*, 21, (2001), 473–492; A. H. Winefield, N. Gillespie, C. Stough et al., 'Occupational stress in

5.4 Influences from Popular Culture

Children's literature does not exist in a vacuum, and it reflects and responds to external events and pressures. The characters and behaviour of fictional academics do not operate in isolation, but mirror historical events and existing structures which are firmly embedded into our culture, responding to and producing what publishers believe will be commercially viable product. The readers of children's literature, too, are part of this experience: 'children's knowledge, understanding, and values are culturally saturated'.[717] Given that half of the corpus has been published in the last 25 years, many fictional academics have absorbed and inherited characteristics from other media.

Haynes has traced the developing stereotype of the scientist in popular culture, suggesting that these function as 'enduring myths to explore and express the deep-rooted but often irrational fears their society has held, usually inarticulately, and perhaps even subconsciously, with respect to science and technology'.[718] Haynes traces how 'the recurrent mutual suspicion between scientists and other members of society was developed and reinforced in Western literature',[719] chronicling the growing and changing stereotype or

Australian university staff: results from a national survey', *International Journal of Stress Management*, 10(1), (2003), 51; J. Schulz, 'The impact of role conflict, role ambiguity and organizational climate on the job satisfaction of academic staff in research-intensive universities in the UK', *Higher Education Research & Development*, 32(3), (2013), 464–478; M. Darabi, A. Macaskill and L. Reidy, 'A qualitative study of the UK academic role: positive features, negative aspects and associated stressors in a mainly teaching-focused university', *Journal of Further and Higher Education*, 41(4), (2017), 566–580.

[717] E. Arizpe and M. Styles, *Children Reading Pictures: Interpreting Visual Texts* (London: Routledge, 2004), p. 87.

[718] Haynes, *From Faust to Strangelove*, p. 313. [719] Ibid., p. 6.

caricature: the oral tradition of the sorcerer or shaman; alchemists (moving beyond areas most people can understand); evil Dr Faustus (the intellectual madman); the foolish Restoration virtuosi ('pursuing useless, irrelevant, and usually disgusting research, into topics with which no gentleman should concern himself'[720]); the Enlightenment philosophers (Newton, and the scientist as genius); the 'Romantic image of the scientist as cold, inhuman, and unable to relate to others' which 'has been one of the most influential in twentieth-century stereotyping of the scientist in both literature and film',[721] particularly in its depiction and exploration of Dr Frankenstein; the Victorian adventurer-scientist who 'should be an isolated individual or at most supported by a small band of assistants, necessarily inferior to him in mental ability';[722] the *fin-de-siècle* adulation of the inventor, and the connection between the scientist and machineries of war. The impersonal and amoral scientist dominates in the twentieth century with a roughly chronological development of 'the power maniac seeking to destroy the world ... the scientist with an essentially evil philosophy ... the scientist as exemplar of amoral perspective ... because of his own personal inadequacies in nonrational pursuits'[723] and finally 'a different kind of troubled and inadequate scientist, a peculiarly twentieth-century figure': the scientist who has lost control of his discovery.[724] These representations coalesce in the aftermath of the atomic bomb[725] and the invention of nuclear power and its associated risks, colouring our modern conception of the fictional scientist. Haynes stresses that men dominate throughout, and that fictional characters such as Dr Faustus, Dr Frankenstein, Dr Moreau, Dr Jekyll, Dr Caligari and Dr Strangelove have done more to influence Western society's perception of scientists than actual scientists (Newton, Curie and Einstein being exceptions), playing out 'Western society's own confused cost–benefit analysis

[720] Ibid., p. 35. [721] Ibid., p. 91. [722] Ibid., p. 141. [723] Ibid., p. 266. [724] Ibid., p. 269.
[725] Ibid., pp. 174–175.

of science, its terrors, and its promises'.[726] This cultural bias towards science and scientists can also point to further reasons for the male dominance within the books: while science itself is dominated by men across all occupations,[727] the supposedly radical and forward-looking genre of science fiction is also notoriously dominated by aggressive and elite male characters.[728] Leading children's books author Ursula Le Guin described science fiction's sexist and hierarchical structure:

> From a social point of view most SF has been incredibly regressive and unimaginative. All those Galactic Empires, taken straight from the British Empire of 1880. All those planets – with 80 trillion miles between them – conceived of as warring nation-states, or as colonies to be exploited, or to be nudged by the benevolent Imperium of Earth towards self-development – the White Man's Burden all over again. The Rotary Club of Alpha Centauri, that's the size of it . . . It is a perfect baboon patriarchy, with the Alpha Male on top, being respectfully groomed, from time to time, by his inferiors.[729]

It can be shown how the previous depiction of academics in children's literature informs the depictions in later texts. In an analysis of the maturing science in the *Professor Branestawm* books, Bell observes that, over time, 'images of science become more ambivalent, drawing on the childlike images of the past while

---

726 Ibid., p. 204. 727 European Commission, 'She Figures 2015', chapter 3.

728 Haynes, *From Faust to Strangelove*, p. 168.

729 U. Le Guin, 'American SF and the Other', *Science Fiction Studies*, 2(3), (November 1975), pp. 209–210.

adding new features'[730] as the 'nostalgic tendencies of book production and dissemination' means that the images portrayed are ones that look 'back nostalgically at the time and remains resonant in its nostalgia today'.[731] The representations of academics we find in children's books become more stereotypical over time, compounding and self-referencing popular fictional figures in children's literature, from the mid-twentieth century onward. Indeed, the academics found in enduring (still in print, or available in multiple editions) or popular (many-selling) children's books from the Victorian period until the middle of the twentieth century set the blueprint for other characters to follow, helping to form the dominant cultural stereotype of academics in children's literature themselves, *The Water-Babies'* Professor Ptthmllnsprts,[732] Professor Branestawm[733] and *The Lion, The Witch and the Wardrobe's* Professor Digory Kirke[734] setting the tone for much literature that followed.

Furthermore, the anti-intellectualism – 'the distrust of intellectuals and the resentment of intellectual activities'[735] shown in picture books such as Professor P. Brain,[736] Professor Poopypants,[737] Professor Bumblebrain[738] and Professor Stupido[739] – has a long history. 'The strain of anti-intellectualism has been a constant thread winding its way through our political and cultural

---

[730] Bell, 'The Incredible Adventurs of Professor Branestawm: The Maturing Image of Science in 20th Century Juvenile Literature', p. 211.

[731] Ibid. [732] Kingsley, *The Water-Babies*.

[733] Hunter, *The Incredible Adventures of Professor Branestawm* onwards.

[734] Lewis, *The Lion, the Witch and the Wardrobe*.

[735] R. Chapman and J. Ciment, *Culture Wars: An Encyclopedia of Issues, Viewpoints and Voices* (New York, NY: Routledge, 2009), p. 27.

[736] McLeay, *Professor P. Brain's Astronomical Trip*.

[737] Pilkey, *Captain Underpants and the Perilous Plot of Professor Poopypants*.

[738] Robb, *Professor Bumblebrain's Bonkers Book on God*.

[739] Griffiths, *39-Story Treehouse*.

life, nurtured by the false notion that democracy means that "my ignorance is just as good as your knowledge."'[740] Described as a 'Cult of Ignorance',[741] anti-intellectual popularist rhetoric has played out in mainstream culture, particularly in American election campaigns. In 1952, Adlai Stevenson was dubbed an 'egghead' by Richard Nixon, and 'this dichotomy carried over into future elections, one candidate serving an as "everyman" and the other, often unfairly, cast as an elitist intellectual'.[742] In 1968, presidential candidate George Wallace, Governor of Alabama, 'got his strongest applause for denouncing bureaucrats, pointy-headed pseudo-intellectuals and professors who know "how to run the war in Vietnam but can't park their bicycles."'[743] Carrying on to the present day, we find UK politicians sneering that they have 'had enough of experts',[744] that 'the suspicion of experts goes back to antiquity and it's a very healthy thing to have. Experts, soothayers and astrologers are in much the same category',[745] and – at time of writing – a President of the United States of America decrying 'fake news' while promoting 'alternative facts' and making statements like 'I love the poorly educated. We're the smartest people, we're the most loyal people'.[746] Given the coverage of this type of statement in

---

[740] Asimov, 'A Cult of Ignorance', p. 19.   [741] Ibid.

[742] Chapman and Ciment, *Culture Wars*, p. 27.

[743] L. Rohler, 'Conservative appeals to the people: George Wallace's populist rhetoric', *Southern Communication Journal*, 64(4), (1999), 316–322, DOI: 10.1080/10417949909373146, p. 322.

[744] Gove, quoted in Mance, 'Britain has had enough of experts, says Gove'.

[745] Rees-Mogg, quoted in P. MacInnes, 'Brits still love a good toff. The ubiquity of Jacob Rees-Mogg proves it', Opinion, *The Guardian* (Monday, 28 November 2016), http://www.theguardian.com/commentisfree/2016/nov/28/jacob-rees-mogg-boris-johnson-ubiquity-toffs.

[746] Trump, quoted in J. Chait, 'The oddly snobbish anti-intellectualism of Donald Trump', *New York Magazine* (26 October 2016), http://nymag.com/daily/intelligencer/2016/10/the-oddly-snobbish-anti-intellectualism-of-donald-trump.html.

popular news media over the past sixty years, anti-intellectualism is now firmly entrenched into western culture,[747] and is seen playing out in children's literature, from the laughter at the lecture in *Sylvie and Bruno*[748] onwards. The academic as baffled failure in children's books reaffirms established tropes, becomes more popular in the latter half of the twentieth century and teaches the next generation to distrust boffins, eggheads and intellectuals. As Franzini, in her study on the representation of intelligence in children's television, notes: 'this lack of emphasis on academics, together with its "uncoolness" underscores our society's devaluation of intelligence, thus keeping intelligence unattractive to people from an early age'.[749] The children most susceptible to this bombardment, of course, are those who do not have the cultural capital (either financial or intellectual) to shield them, and who are not encouraged to partake in higher education despite these prevailing cultural messages.

There is, in addition, a double whammy for *female* experts, given the 'concerted and ubiquitous … attacks on women and on women's credibility' in the modern media environment;[750] and the popular media's attitude to women, and the lack of their representation, also provides another sociological driver for their exclusion in any corpus-based

---

[747] Lecklider: *Inventing the Egghead*; T. Nichols, 'The Death of Expertise', *The Federalist* (17 January 2014), http://thefederalist.com/2014/01/17/the-death-of-expertise/; Tobolowsky and Reynolds (eds.), *Anti-Intellectual Representations of American Colleges and Universities*.

[748] Carroll, *Sylvie and Bruno*.

[749] Franzini, 'Is School Cool? Representations of Academics and Intelligence on Teen Television', p. 198

[750] L. Gilmore, *Tainted Witness. Why We Doubt What Women Say About Their Lives* (New York, NY: Columbia University Press, 2017), p. 22.

research. Biases exist as to expectations of who is allowed to be a genius, reflecting prevailing gender stereotypes.[751] Children's media is far from the only media that is biased against women, in a problem that is world-wide and ongoing.[752] Children's literature begins from a world of inherited anti-female bias, although it should be awake, by now, to this, given the volume of research that demonstrates its complicity.

Illustrators, authors and publishers draw on a cultural inheritance comprising alchemists, wizards, the music-hall, popular literature, film and television. We also see a presumption in children's literature that academia equates to scientific enquiry, and scientific enquiry equates to male domination, which is something that has both been picked up from the history of academic institutions and reinforced by cultural stereotypes: the highlighted shorthand of modern's children's fiction, which 'depends upon a canon of sentiment'.[753] The

---

[751] K. C. Elmore and M. Luna-Lucero, 'Light Bulbs or Seeds? How Metaphors for Ideas Influence Judgments about Genius', *Social Psychological and Personality Science*, (2016), 1948550616667611.

[752] S. Macharia, L. Ndangam, M. Saboor et al., 'Who makes the news? Global media monitoring project 2015', World Association for Christian Communication (WACC), (2015), http://cdn.agilitycms.com/who-makes-the-news/Imported/reports_2015/highlights/highlights_en.pdf; M. J. Michel, 'Racial and gender diversity of the characters in The New Yorker cartoons', *Proceedings of the Natural Institute of Science*, 2(6), (2015), http://pnis.co/vol2/h6.html; T. Underwood and D. Bamman, 'The Gender Balance of Fiction, 1800–2007' (2016), https://tedunderwood.com/2016/12/28/the-gender-balance-of-fiction-1800-2007/; Women in Media, 'Mates over Merit, The Women in Media Report – A study of gender differences in Australian media' Media, Entertainment, and Arts Alliance, 2016 www.womeninmedia.net/wp-content/uploads/2017/10/Mates-Over-Merit_full-report.pdf.

[753] Stevenson, 'Sentiment and significance: the impossibility of recovery in the children's literature canon, or The Drowning of The Water-Babies', p. 112.

dominant form of the professor in children's literature that we arrive at by the close of the twentieth century is, then, a postmodern repacking of various themes, tropes and influences, which, like postmodern art,

> splices high and low culture, it raids and parodies past art, it questions all absolutes, it swamps reality in a culture of recycled images, it has to do with deconstruction, with consumerism, with television and the information society.[754]

It can be very difficult to break these associations, once made: they can be played with, overridden or deliberately challenged, but 'Many, if not all of us, work in systems in which books published some time in the past are used regularly'[755] and 'The system is older than you. It has absorbed more venom than you can ever hope to emit.'[756] We have to choose to understand our ongoing inheritance from children's literature in order to challenge it.

5.5 Conclusion

These three distinct tropes in the corpus – the teacher, the baffled inventor and the evil genius madman – have evolved over time, and now dominate the behaviour of academics in children's literature. The stereotypes of professors and doctors themselves become functional aspects of children's literature, and are entrenched by the time the majority of the corpus has been created from established stereotypes embedded into contemporary culture, in an act of 'Cultural Cloning'[757]

---

[754] P. Brooker, *Modernism/Postmodernism* (London: Routledge, 2014), p. 3.

[755] Peterson and Lach, 'Gender Stereotypes in Children's Books', p. 188.

[756] J. Crispin, *Why I am Not a Feminist: A Feminist Manifesto* (London: Melville House, 2017), p. 13.

[757] P. Essed and D. T. Goldberg, 'Cloning cultures: the social injustices of sameness', *Ethnic and Racial Studies*, 25(6), (2002), 1066–1082.

which is predicated on the taken-for-granted desirability of certain types, the often-unconscious tendency to comply with normative standards, the easiness with the familiar and the subsequent rejection of those who are perceived as deviant.[758]

It is easy, and in places just, to decry these as pejorative or hollow depictions of intellectual achievement and the academy. We also have to concede that these stereotypes work because they are so suitable for their audience:

it is difficult to ... overcome the present negative image. Because upper primary age children delight in slapstick and exaggerated humor, the character of the 'Mad Scientist' is tailor-made for them.[759]

However, these stereotypes now also provide a framework in which modern authors and illustrators can swiftly introduce characters into children's literature, without the need for lengthy explanation or backstory: Knapman commented that Dr Frankenstinker came from 'rooting around in the dressing up box of children's literature';[760] Grey said, 'stereotyping characters is a way of staying within the bounds of what seems normal to the reader'.[761] While this does not excuse the bias and lack of diversity we see, it raises questions about the nature, role, function and necessity of stereotypes, which fulfil 'cognitive,

---

[758] Ibid., p. 1070.

[759] J. E. McAdam, 'The persistent stereotype: children's images of scientists', *Physics Education*, 25, (1990), 102–105, p. 104.

[760] Knapman, personal communication, February 2017.

[761] Grey, personal communication, February 2017.

emotional, and pragmatic' functions.[762] While stereotypes are normally 'treated in conjunction with prejudice',[763] children's literature depends on their advantages: stable relationships, constructs and meanings in which the 'brevity of description and extreme poverty of detail permit an immediate recognition of the basic model',[764] participating 'in the elaboration of the text as network, in a reworking of models and problematization of commonplace visions of the world'.[765] This analysis has attempted to unpack the complex historical and societal trends which underpin the stereotypes of professors that exist in children's literature.

An attempt to describe how we can build upon this knowledge positively is given in Section 6.

6 Conclusion

This analysis has undertaken a major publishing history of the representation of academia, and academics, in children's literature, scoping out the history, growth, positioning and representation of academia in books written for a childhood audience, analysing their collective book culture. A strict methodology was developed to build a longitudinal corpus, excluding books that developed as spin-offs from other media: however, the resulting corpus has been shown to be increasingly intertextual, referring to, and building on, other

---

[762] A. Schaff, 'The pragmatic function of stereotypes', *International Journal of the Sociology of Language*, 45, (1984), 89–100, p. 89.

[763] R. D. Ashmore and F. K. Del Boca, 'Conceptual approaches to stereotypes and stereotyping', in D. Hamilton (ed.), *Cognitive Processes in Stereotyping and Intergroup Behavior* (London: Psychology Press, 1981), pp. 1–35, p. 10.

[764] R. Amossy and T. Heidingsfeld, 'Stereotypes and representation in fiction', *Poetics Today*, 5(4), (1984), pp. 689–700, p. 695.

[765] Ibid., p. 700.

media and popular culture, and these internal and external influences on how the academy is represented in children's literature have been teased out. The trope of the male, mad, muddlehead has been shown to have condensed and stabilised within children's illustrated books towards the end of the twentieth century, and is now a known and readily identifiable stereotype. The white-haired old scientist, called SomethingStupid, is a vehicle and mechanism within children's picture and illustrated books, which has a complex relationship to the real-life academy.

Throughout this analysis, the fictional university depicted in children's literature has been closely compared with historical and current statistics about its real-world counterpart. We have shown that the real university has both historical and present issues regarding diversity, including gender balance, race and class. With some of those – such as gender balance – improving slowly over the past decade or so, we hope that other media referencing this culture should also begin to reflect these changes, even if it will take time for this to trickle down (the growth of the female professoriate in children's literature being much slower than we would expect; see Section 4.4). With other equally complex diversity issues – such as race and class within the academy and the elitism of high-performing institutions combined with their cultural dominance – can we really complain if children's literature does not reflect a fairer world than our real-life institutions? These factors do not exist in isolation, and children's literature has held up a mirror to the university, reflecting what it has shown, darkly, indicating that 'Illustrations and texts in books for young children ... both carry and challenge prevailing cultural ideologies and stereotypes'.[766] The dominant historical representation of academics in popular culture is that of old white scientific men: combatting this is a weight for any author or

---

[766] Spitz, *Inside Picture Books*, p. 21.

illustrator to lift, while also assumptions and tropes that have been learnt by even a young readership on the mechanics and function of professors and doctors within children's literature need to be taken into account. It will take playful imagination and deliberate action by publishers, authors and illustrators to decompress the stereotype of the male, mad, muddlehead that the academy has been distilled to, particularly in picture books, and this may never happen if the university sector itself does not improve on its own diversity measures.

Given the work necessary to gather the corpus, it is highly unlikely that any children would have seen all of the examples presented here,[767] but they will have come across enough (in books, but also in other media) to understand the ineffectual mad male professor stereotype, given 'children and their culture are shaped not just by individual texts but by the aggregate impact of all children's literature, especially the most popular or most recommended works'.[768] The long tradition of anti-intellectualism, as well as racism and sexism, in children's literature lives on in previously published texts, and will be encountered by children in higher volumes than any modern publishing attempts to address or subvert problematic stereotypes. The effect this will have on a child reader is debateable; however, it is likely (given studies that have been carried out on the effect of other stereotypes) that children will internalise the negative messages regarding intellectual achievement, expertise and higher education that they are being mostly shown. We have to ask, 'What values are being promoted, and who is the reader to become – whose life are

---

[767] Except my own.

[768] B. L. Clark, 'Introduction', in B. L. Clark and M. R. Higonnet (eds.), *Girls*, *Boys*, *Books*, *Toys: Gender in Children's Literature and Culture* (Baltimore MD: Johns Hopkins University Press, 1999), pp. 1–10, p. 6.

you sharing – during the reading?'[769] When we trot out examples of the male, mad, muddlehead 'What are we doing to – or not doing for – children?'[770] How does the role and effect of children's literature fit into the complex media landscape that contributes to children's development? It has been shown that 'career aspirations of young men and women are shaped by societal stereotypes about gender' and 'by the age of 6, girls are less likely than boys to believe their gender are "really really smart", because "cultural messages about the presumed cognitive abilities of males and females are likely to be influential throughout development"' in a paper titled *Gender Stereotypes About Intellectual Ability Emerge Early and Influence Children's Interests*.[771] Is it coincidental that around the age of six is when most children begin to read? This analysis provides evidence that academia and intellectual achievement is presented in a sexist, racist way in children's books, and Bian et al.'s study confirms that this is contributing to gender disparities in science and academia, which has ramifications throughout academic structures for female intellectual attainment.[772] Stereotypes impair women's careers in science,[773] and probably do so for other minorities in other situations, too. Time out, authors, illustrators and publishers!

What would challenging the stereotypes revealed in this analysis entail? Indeed, what would it take to break the overall bias towards able-bodied white

---

[769] Doonan, *Looking at Pictures in Picture Books*, p. 50.

[770] Rose, *The Case of Peter Pan, or The Impossibility of Children's Fiction*, p. x.

[771] L. Bian, S. J. Leslie and A. Cimpian, 'Gender stereotypes about intellectual ability emerge early and influence children's interests', *Science*, 355(6323), (2017), 389–391, p. 389.

[772] European Commission, 'She Figures 2015'.

[773] E. Reuben, P. Sapienza and L. Zingales, 'How stereotypes impair women's careers in science', *Proceedings of the National Academy of Sciences*, 111(12), (2014), 4403–4408.

men in children's literature? More females – behaving in both good and bad ways – and in particular more *elderly* females; less gendering of even inanimate objects as male; more black, Asian or ethnic minority characters; fewer upper middle or upper class characters; more attention to diverse depictions of physical disability; avoidance of ableist depictions of mental illness; and less reinforcement of heteronormative behaviour, would start to redress the imbalance shown within this particular corpus, in a shopping list that could be applied to almost any genre or topic in children's literature, to make it more closely and fairly reflect societal makeup while providing diverse role models that can help positively shape culture and behaviour. Expanding the role in fiction for experts and professors by playing with these variables would allow an expansion of a depiction of the professoriate which has become increasingly narrow in the latter half of the twentieth century. However, is it realistically possible to change this, given the challenges that this poses to publisher, author, illustrator and reader in fighting against a complex and tightly bound cultural inheritance and a well-defined marketplace? The quantification of biases via content analysis, which serves to highlight the lack of diversity in children's literature, has been a focus of much academic activity for the past forty years, but we see here that these biases maintain, persist and even grow. Any modern trends in encouraging diversity

> and decreased stereotyping cannot be taken for granted and probably reflects real gains in public consciousness . . . about the importance of gender-egalitarian displays in children's media. Antifeminist backlash in other media . . . suggest that such a trend is reversible.[774]

[774] Clark, Guilmain, Saucier and Tavarez, 'Two Steps Forward, One Step Back', p. 446.

From a methods perspective, this study raises interesting opportunities for the study of children's literature, particularly for those undertaking longitudinal corpus-based research. Indeed, this research is an advert for transparency and the use of digital media within the research process, given that it would not exist without its trajectory from discussions on Twitter to a collection on Tumblr to blog post to write-up. Methodological innovations include highlighting the importance of liaising with librarians when undertaking a study of this nature; the integration of library records and datasets into longitudinal study, expanding the methodology of current approaches in children's literature (although it is conceded that much more could be done to both improve and visualise the British National Bibliography data[775]); the use of online environments, including social media resources, which have been demonstrated to be a rich information source to complement existing, and essential, library catalogues; the integration of digitised content, and content created by digitisation on demand, which can be juxtaposed with the consultation of physical texts, to undertake a longitudinal content analysis and expand the set of available books to study(while also making source material available as an anthology[776]); and the need to develop methodological approaches to encompass print-on-demand or ebook-only publications, when studying the modern children's literature publishing environment. It was only possible to build the broad corpus analysed here by using an array of digital methods, online resources, digitisation

---

[775] This is a much larger project than the one described here, and the children's literature community is encouraged to liaise with librarians to begin working towards the availability of national bibliographies of children's literature, derived, checked and authorised from existing national bibliography sources, to allow data-led analysis of the field to be undertaken. Until such datasets are created, it is difficult to pursue further data-driven analysis, given that there are too many areas of concern and confusion in the existing datasets.

[776] Terras, *The Professor in Children's Literature: An Anthology*

on demand and social media platforms, indicating the centrality of the digital to future children's literature research. There are no doubt further research gains to be found by undertaking large-scale automated analysis of the actual texts within children's literature corpora, although the copyright restrictions in gaining access to enough text, and the complexities of semantic image processing, mean that this is a further, rather than nearer, future research methodology. It is one to keep in mind, however, given developments in big data analysis for other media.[777]

As well as these methodological benefits of digital approaches and use of the online information environment, it may be that creative use of online mechanisms can help broadcast and challenge bias in children's literature in a far wider way than can traditional subscription-only behind-paywall academic publications. It is not enough to tell other academics about the biases involved, but to involve authors, illustrators, publishers and ultimately consumers of children's literature in the debates surrounding diversity and stereotyping. We see this in online activism springing up in social media campaigns contesting the lack of diversity, or enforced gender roles, of different media, such as #OscarsSoWhite[778] and #LetToysBeToys,[779] or those which respond to structural oppression in higher education such as #DistractinglySexy, #StayMadAbby and #BeckyWithTheBadGrades,[780] which 'exemplify an

---

[777] M. Terras, J. Baker, J. Hetherington et al., 'Enabling complex analysis of large-scale digital collections: humanities research, high-performance computing, and transforming access to British Library digital collections', *Digital Scholarship in the Humanities* (2017), https://doi.org/10.1093/llc/fqx020.

[778] KnowYourMeme, 'Oscars so white' (2016), http://knowyourmeme.com/memes/oscars-so-white.

[779] http://lettoysbetoys.org.uk/

[780] For an overview see A. Morrison, 'Making fun of injustice: hashtags, humour, and collective action online', in D. Parry and C. Johnson (eds.), *Digital Dilemmas:*

emerging mode of online resistance by marginalized subjects' with 'the use of social media platforms to gain wide visibility, the creation of hashtags to allow for grassroots collective participation and viral spread of content, and, crucially, the use of humour to destabilize the institutional framing of these conflicts by dominant groups'.[781] Content analysis done by volunteers provides research as ammunition; for example, the *VIDA Count*,[782] which quantifies gender disparity in major literary publications and book reviews. Academic and industry reports on bias are accruing, such as those from the *Geena Davis Institute on Gender in Media*,[783] which focusses on the film and television industry, the outputs of the *Cooperative Children's Book Center* at the University of Wisconsin-Madison,[784] which produce yearly statistics on children's books about people of colour and first/native nations,[785] and the UK Arts Council funded 'Survey of Ethnic Representation Within UK Children's Literature 2017' produced by the Centre for Literacy in Primary Education.[786] It is clear that digital, community-based participatory methods will be part of the solution to broadcast, share and challenge assumptions regarding what is appropriate in children's literature, and this development is evident in sites such

Transforming Gender Identities and Power Relations in Everyday Life (Palgrave MacMillan, Forthcoming). Accepted. 34 ms pp.

[781] Ibid., p. 1. [782] www.vidaweb.org/the-count [783] https://seejane.org/

[784] https://ccbc.education.wisc.edu/default.asp

[785] K. T. Horning, 'Publishing statistics on children's books about people of color and first/native nations and by people of color and first/native nations authors and illustrators', documented by the Cooperative Children's Book Center School of Education, University of Wisconsin-Madison (2016), https://ccbc.education.wisc.edu/books/pcstats.asp.

[786] Centre for Literacy in Primary Education (CLPE), 'Survey of Ethnic Representation within UK Children's Literature 2017' (2018) clpe.org.uk/library-and-resources/research/reflecting-realities-survey-ethnic-representation-within-uk-children.

as *A Mighty Girl*,[787] 'The world's largest collection of books, toys and movies for smart, confident, and courageous girls' (2017), and *We Need Diverse Books*,[788]

> a grassroots organization of children's book lovers that advocates essential changes in the publishing industry to produce and promote literature that reflects and honors the lives of all young people. (n. d.)

Indeed, the 'most funded book in crowdfunding history' is an inspirational collection of '100 bedtime stories about the life of 100 extraordinary women from the past and the present, illustrated by 60 female artists from all over the world':[789] *Good Night Stories for Rebel Girls*.[790] Raising over $1m from 20,000 backers through a Kickstarter and Indiegogo campaign, the success of this project shows that the authors 'are filling a vacuum . . . We are responding to clear need',[791] which should also be a rejoinder to those who say there is no market for diverse children's books.[792] The follow-up volume, *Good Night Stories for Rebel Girls Vol. 2*,[793] crowdfunding at the time of writing, has gone on to 'smash the Kickstarter record for the fastest-funded publishing project in

[787] www.amightygirl.com [788] http://weneeddiversebooks.org/

[789] Rebel Girls, Home page (2017), www.rebelgirls.co, accessed 19 June 2017.

[790] Favilli and Cavallo, *Good Night Stories for Rebel Girls*.

[791] Favilli, quoted in J. Rosen, 'Kids' book for "Rebel Girls" tops $1m in crowdfunding', *Publisher's Weekly* (15 September 2016), www.publishersweekly.com/pw/by-topic/childrens/childrens-book-news/article/71485-kids-book-for-rebel-girls-tops-1m-in-crowdfunding.html.

[792] J. Taxel, 'Children's literature at the turn of the century: toward a political economy of the publishing industry', *Research in the Teaching of English* (2002), pp. 145–197.

[793] Favilli and Cavallo, *Good Night Stories for Rebel Girls*.

the crowdfunding platform's history'.[794] It would appear that the current digital environment is finally matching demand for diverse texts with commercial distribution mechanisms which can allow them to be profitable. However, concerns remain that the market is for texts which prioritise female empowerment only, rather than equality and diversity across the board.[795]

Can publishers do more to foster, encourage and respond to this type of activity? Despite the comments made earlier about digital-only print-on-demand texts, and while recognising the skill it takes to produce high-quality children's literature, it should also be possible for authors, illustrators and publishing houses to experiment with a wider range of titles, exploring diverse issues and harnessing the power of social media, if using online publishing mechanisms. There needs to be concerted effort in utilising online platforms to disrupt established publishing hegemonies, and reaching and reflecting wide audiences, while counteracting the low-quality, rushed digital content flooding the market, as a mechanism to embrace the forces of social media that are encouraging open discussions on diversity and difference.[796] Digital participation and critique of children's literature from diverse communities could also provide a necessary feedback loop to the publishing industry, much in the way online discourse is now influencing

---

[794] R. Ruiz, '"Good Night Stories for Rebel Girls" takes Kickstarter by storm – again', *Mashable* (20 June 2017), http://mashable.com/2017/06/20/good-night-stories-for-rebel-girls-volume-2-kickstarter/#rQK5YBKgFSqH.

[795] A. Hill, '"Queens just look out of windows": how children's books are failing to show gender equality', *Guardian, Family* (9 September 2017), www.theguardian.com/lifeandstyle/2017/sep/09/queens-just-look-out-of-windows-how-childrens-books-are-failing-to-show-gender-equality.

[796] For an overview of other online resources see P. Nel, '"The boundaries of imagination"; or, the all-white world of children's books, 2014', *Nine Kinds of Pie, Philip Nel's Blog* (17 March 2014), www.philnel.com/2014/03/17/boundaries/.

television production,[797] or in the shift in producer and consumer power demonstrated with the growth of the fan fiction community.[798] This digital outreach need not only be online, to avoid the 'excessive dependence' on the Internet, to improve digital literacy in impoverished rural areas worldwide.[799] Engaging with this digital shift will also require 'new media modes of public/scholarship' which

> offer us the opportunity and the imperative to transform ourselves as scholars, because our technologies and practices remain shot through with systemic biases and inequities that structure and constrain existing educational, social, political, and economic interactions and institutions. How could they not be?[800]

This text has aimed to be transparent in the presentation of research activities, including the labour involved in the publishing process, whilst being respectful of the efforts made by others other than the writer which were required to present it to you, in this form. The text you are reading here is published in print, but is also freely available in online 'open access'

---

[797] S. M. Falero, *Digital Participatory Culture and the TV Audience* (Springer, 2016).

[798] L. Miller, 'You Belong to Me: The fanfiction boom is reshaping the power dynamic between creators and consumers', *Vulture.com* (11 March 2015), www.vulture.com/2015/03/fanfiction-guide.html#essay.

[799] R. K. Gairola and A. Datta, 'Portable India: a vision of responsible literacy in digital democracy', *Advocate* (7 October 2015), http://gcadvocate.com/2015/10/07/portable-india-a-vision-of-responsible-literacy-in-digital-democracy/.

[800] A. Morrison, 'Of, by, and for the Internet: new media studies and public scholarship', in J. Sayers (ed.), *Routledge Companion to Digital Media Studies* (Routledge, 2017), pp. 56–66, p. 64.

to anyone who wishes to read it. This was a policy decision regarding the necessity to make such criticism available in order to reach a wide community, in the hope that the investment needed for open access means it can contribute to ongoing debates on gender, diversity, higher education and the media created for children. However, this was only possible through UCL paying a Book Processing Charge of £6,762, and I am cognisant of the privilege this represents, and the open access advantages it endows. It is hoped that, by making such a forward-looking longitudinal study freely available to all, it can contribute to discussions regarding media and higher education and provide an accessible resource to bolster future ongoing discussion.

There are, of course, weaknesses in this study. The corpus has been treated as a whole, when it is unlikely that any author, illustrator or publisher will have come into contact with many of the representations mentioned here, and it should be remembered that these characters are created from a complex relationship with prior influences. Academics in pre-teen periodicals were included, and although there is a confidence in the exhaustion of candidates in books found by this particular methodology, there will be some that have been missed, and more can be done to ensure that the coverage of comics is comprehensive, given how patchy their documentation is. A bibliometric method could have been developed to track recurrent characters across book series, rather than noting only their first appearance in the corpus. There has been no attempt at 'reader response criticism' in discerning the child reader's experience of this corpus.[801] There is always a danger of becoming too po-faced about media which is designed to – and does – entertain children, and we have

---

[801] J.P. Tompkins, *Reader-Response Criticism: From Formalism to Post-Structuralism* (Baltimore: Johns Hopkins University Press 1980) Discussions with my own children were not methodical.

to remember that the slapstick humour of the baffled expert, or the world-destroying naughtiness of the madman, works for children because they are stereotypes that are ridiculous and funny, and that play with behavioural expectations and norms: it is hoped that this has been noted throughout the text, without falling too hard into stern potholes of Lacanian and Jungian symbolism. Further research is needed into the impact of the stereotypical representation of intellect and academic achievement before conclusions can be drawn about the effect they have on children, although all signs point to media diets impacting behaviour and children's self-belief and self-actuation. Obvious follow-on studies can be sketched out: how universities and academics are portrayed in texts for older child audiences that are not illustrated,[802] or a comparison of how the representation of academics in English children's texts compares with books in other languages.[803] There is more that could be, and should be, done with the British National Bibliography dataset, including further cleaning and double-checking data and examples, in order to build up a public-facing informational resource that would benefit a wide-ranging children's literature community. Distant Reading could be expanded to the content of texts, rather than limited to their metadata, although copyright is a barrier here.

Thought must be given into how best to communicate these findings to the authors, illustrators and publishers that create children's literature, who can maintain stereotypes, or have the mechanisms and potential to create products

---

[802] I call dibs.

[803] Seventy-one texts have been found in languages other than English that contain an illustrated Professor. The most methodical search undertaken has been within texts in the Dutch language, where 27 professors were found: 26 are mostly old, white-haired, scientific, baffled and evil men, and one is a female child. It is likely that these stereotypes are widespread, internationally. Many have been found so far in children's literature in French.

that can challenge problematic representation. How best can we persuade the consumers of children's literature (or, more accurately, the *purchasers* of children's literature) to point their spending power to books that can entertain, while not excluding a diverse range of readers or have the effect of narrowing their opportunities? These last two points are no small ask, and it is hoped that, by carrying out this study in such a public-facing manner right from its inception, others can become aware of the problems that exist regarding representation in children's literature, while also wagging a finger at the academy itself for its own problematic behaviour regarding diversity. Time out, provosts and chancellors – 85 percent of whom, across Europe, are white men![804] It's complicated,[805] but a range of practical interventions can be used to improve gender equality in research organisations.[806]

In some respects, this topic has been a tiny borehole through the pantheon of children's literature, showing how it upholds structural inequalities and systemic biases that are entrenched within society, while simultaneously mocking and criticising the world it reflects through stressing the ridiculousness of the stereotypes it builds upon. Authors, illustrators and publishers can be censured for profiting from negative stereotypes without creatively or imaginatively challenging them; however, they can also use these ready-made constructs as scaffolding upon which to build plot and pace, without using up precious resources in explanation. While the stereotypes

---

[804] European University Association, 'More women become university leaders – equality still far away' (13 May 2016), www.eua.be/activities-services/news/news item/2016/05/13/more-women-become-university-leaders–equality-still-far-away.

[805] European Commission, 'She Figures 2015'.

[806] Science Europe, 'Science Europe practical guide to improving gender equality in research organisations' (2017), www.scienceeurope.org/wp-content/uploads/2017/01/SE_Gender_Practical-Guide.pdf.

presented from this analysis can be and should justly be questioned, the dual nature of (particularly present-day) children's literature in both reinforcing and highlighting cultural tropes needs to be situated within the postmodern context. There are tensions between the relationship of real life to children's fiction, the depiction of accurate representations, the genesis of pejorative stereotypes that reaffirm social bias while showing how problematic they are, or the development of hopeful and imaginative representations that can challenge established tropes. We see all this wrestling within the corpus, in an attempt to educate and entertain children, in media that depend upon cultural shorthand for efficiency. Children's literature scholarship depends on spotting these intersections:

> Young children need plenty of time to sort out the differences between make-believe and reality, dreaming and living, fantasy and fact. To recognize this is to pay attention to the form and content of the imagery we make available to them. It is to understand that, from their point of view, each image has an effect that we as adults do not fully grasp, unless, perhaps, we pay attention.[807]

It is hoped that, by paying close attention to the representation of one profession within children's literature, future debates on higher education, public perceptions of the academy and the impact of media created for children that deals with intellectual achievement and agency can all be considered anew.

The asking of a simple question – how are universities depicted in children's illustrated literature? – has resulted in a multifaceted analysis of

---

[807] Spitz, *Inside Picture Books*, p. 208.

visual and textual tropes, evolving into a picture of intertextuality, popular culture, the mechanisms that create and utilise stereotypes and the relationship of the fictional academy to its real-world counterpart. A study of fictional academics has forced reflection on obsession, intellect, expertise and how professors in the higher education environment are perceived, and also how they operate. This has both revealed representations of, and been carried out because of, the detail-driven, curiously 'other', mentality that drives many academics and their studies. This is also research that has only been possible because of, and enabled by, a certain amount of privilege. I mean, who would voluntarily spend four years collecting books that feature mad professors in order to make a spreadsheet that counted their beards? And then write a book about it, for fun? Weirdo. Weirdos, the lot of them.,

Acknowledgements

This was not a book I intended to write. In the spring of 2012, while reading to my sons, the eldest of whom was then three years old, and his one-year-old twin brothers, I came across two professors in children's books in quick succession. An initial sharing of these characters on the social media platform Twitter[1] gradually became a habit, and eventually the encouragement came that I should set up a Tumblr blog to collate them,[2] which I duly did: http://academiainchildrenspicturebooks.tumblr.com/.

Searching for mentions of representations of academics in children's books became the thing I did in boring staff meetings, but as well as building what turned out to be a corpus, it allowed me to play with the digital information structures that underpin academic humanities research. My day job at the time of writing was to teach digitisation technologies within a Library school, and I partake in large-scale team-based digital humanities initiatives that aim to open up access to resources through digitisation (such as Transcribe Bentham[3] or the

---

[1] M. Terras, Tweet: 'The Boy's new @octonauts book has this entire academic malarkey down to a tee http://img.ly/hbr3', *Twitter*, 21 April 2012(a), https://twitter.com/melissaterras/status/193762482496602112; M. Terras, Tweet: 'Another top depiction of academia in a kids book http://img.ly/hMcI (Dr Seuss, "Did I ever tell you how lucky you are")', *Twitter*, 3 May 2012(b), https://twitter.com/melissaterras/status/197964592364797952. Unfortunately, Twitter removed rival image hosting services from its apps in September 2012, and so the photos contained within these tweets are no longer are available online.

[2] S. Werner, Tweet: '@melissaterras Yes, you should do that tumblr!', *Twitter*, 2 October 2012, https://twitter.com/wynkenhimself/status/253221046826704896.

[3] http://blogs.ucl.ac.uk/transcribe-bentham/; see also T. Causer and M. Terras, 'Crowdsourcing Bentham: Beyond the Traditional Boundaries of Academic History', *International Journal of Humanities and Arts Computing*, 8(1) (2014), pp. 46–64, http://dx.doi.org/10.3366/ijhac.2014.0119.

Great Parchment Book[4]). Here, instead, was a miniature, unfunded, refreshing project I could undertake on my own, that asked: how do you find difficult-to-trace examples in an under-catalogued and under-digitised area? How exactly do you find representations of universities in children's literature, and which information science methods and approaches are the most fruitful in this changing library environment? The response to writing up my findings in an initial blog post in 2014[5] made it obvious that this wasn't a 'funny-ha-ha' project anymore. An invitation to discuss my work with the Children's Literature Group while visiting Deakin University in Melbourne at the close of 2014 was my first real contact with children's literature scholars, and they encouraged me to think that my research was brave and innovative, and could be useful to others: thus the methodical analysis began. I attempted to finalise this in a paper in 2016, but there was far too much to say. This Element is the result of a playful asking of a question – how is academia represented in children's illustrated books? – answered over a period of a few years, being the result of 'slow' research[6] with no deadlines, no pressures and no funders to answer to, carried out in rare breaks and breathers, for pure ludic joy. Academics are strange like that.

I've leant heavily on the expertise of my colleagues, often ending a meeting about something else with a pointed question about woodcuts in the nineteenth century, or cataloguing guidelines in the twentieth, and I am indebted to those who took the time to listen to me babble about a project seemingly unconnected to the day job. Anne Welsh has been my go-to bibliographer, and 'my' librarian,

---

[4] www.greatparchmentbook.org; see also K. Pal, N. Avery, P. Boston et al., 'Digitally reconstructing the Great Parchment Book: 3D recovery of fire-damaged historical documents', *Digital Scholarship in the Humanities*, 32(4) (1 December 2017), https://academic.oup.com/dsh/article/2670757/Digitally-reconstructing-the-Great-Parchment-Book, accessed 1 May 2018.

[5] Terras, 'Male, Mad and Muddle-Headed: Academics in Children's Picture Books'; Terras, 'Male, Mad and Muddleheaded' (Impact Blog); Parr, 'The Scholarly Web'.

[6] M. Berg and B. Seeber, *The Slow Professor: Challenging the Culture of Speed in the Academy* (University of Toronto Press, 2016).

Acknowledgements

throughout this project. Deb Verhoeven has been a great ally in encouraging my feminist thinking, and she facilitated contact with Professor Clare Bradford and her Children's Literature Seminar colleagues at Deakin University who took the time to discuss my embryonic work, and persuaded me it was worth pursuing further. It was Edward Vanhoutte who suggested that this project was not a blog post but a short book, Lisa Jardine who encouraged it, and Melanie Ramdarshan Bold and Samantha Rayner who gave me the opportunity to publish in this form, with assistance from Bex Lyons. Pauline Reynolds, Lesley Pitman, Claire Easingwood and Julianne Nyhan all provided detailed, insightful comments on an early draft that aided the shaping of my argument. Lorna Richardson was extremely helpful in an initial formatting of the appendices, and Eugene Giddens expertly steered the text to the final version you see here, assisted by Tim Mason, Richard Hallas, Dave Morris, Victoria Parrin and Bethany Thomas from Cambridge University Press.

Tania Evans was my remote assistant in checking details in books at the National Library of Australia, and Floor Buschenhenke assisted with texts in The Koninklijke Bibliotheek in Den Haag. Books were provided for me, digitised on demand, by: Cambridge University Library; The School of Oriental and African Studies Library; University of New Brunswick Library; Watkinson Library, Trinity College, Hartford, Connecticut; Oxford University Libraries; The British Newspaper Archive; and Rare Books and Special Collections, Northern Illinois University Libraries. I would like to thank the anonymous librarians and photographers involved in connecting me with the texts required throughout this project.

I have asked questions of people in the children's literature industry, who replied generously and promptly, including Debbie Foy (Managing Editor of Wayland) and the authors Mavis Crispin, Felice Holman, Mini Grey, Timothy Knapman, Sally Odgers and David Orme, and the illustrator Emily Arnold McCully. Many other information professionals, librarians and academics have aided and abetted, including: James Baker, Giles Bergel, Alan Danskin, Amy Earhart, Graeme Forbes, Vanessa Freedman, Amanda Gailey, Adam Gibson, Ann Gow, Graham Hawley, Graham Hogg, Darryl Mead, Victoria Morris,

Acknowledgements

Aimée Morrison, Ben O'Steen, Lesley Pitman, Ernesto Priego, Melanie Ramdarshan Bold, Samantha Rayner, Pauline Reynolds, Helen Roberts, John Scally, Matthew Symonds, Ben Taylor, Helen Vincent and Sarah Werner. Julianne Nyhan has provided welcome and consistent encouragement, input and supportive friendship throughout the writing of this text. Thank you all for providing helpful advice and further suggestions.

This research was unfunded; however, it was finally completed as part of a scheduled term-long sabbatical from UCL. I'm appreciative of the academic freedom which has allowed me to pursue something outside my normal area of expertise, as well as the support of UCL Library staff, and the UCL resources which have enabled this text to be made available in open access.

I am lucky with my friendships, and thank Felicity and Sattam Al-Mugheiry, Jane Audas, David Beaumont, Natalie Curtis, Claire Easingwood, Susan Edwards, Andrew Green, Hannah Isher, Inna Kizhner, Sue Mucieniks, Fleur Porter, Rosalind Porter, Justin Pniower, Caroline Sills and Edward Vanhoutte for all patiently listening to me bang on about obscure academic characters when they simply asked me how I was. Raj Chand, Cindy McIntyre and Rachel Luck have literally put me back on my feet numerous times during the writing of this text: thank you. I am indebted to my family: my parents, my grandmother, my brother Robin and my cousin Fiona. My husband Andrew Ostler (Os) is the best thing I ever found on the Internet, and this Element would not exist without his practical, intellectual and emotional support.

Finally, thanks go to my children. My eldest, Anthony, excitedly ran home from infant school to present me with doctors and professors in reading books that would not have been found any other way. We have laughed wholeheartedly at Dr Xargle's underfrillies and stinkfume, along with my youngest two, Edward and Fergusson, who gave me surprising insights into their view of texts, in a reminder that, although this is now a serious endeavour, it stems from – and should also be – fun. I have enjoyed every minute of sharing these books with you three: thanks, boys.

For Anthony, Edward and Fergusson (who are turning out to be useful research assistants).

Cambridge Elements

Publishing and Book Culture

Series Editor:
Samantha Rayner
University College London

Samantha Rayner is a Reader in UCL's Department of Information Studies. She is also Director of UCL's Centre for Publishing, co-Director of the Bloomsbury CHAPTER (Communication History, Authorship, Publishing, Textual Editing and Reading) and co-editor of the Academic Book of the Future BOOC (Book as Open Online Content) with UCL Press.

Associate Editor:
Rebecca Lyons
University of Bristol

Rebecca Lyons is a Teaching Fellow at the University of Bristol. She is also co-editor of the experimental BOOC (Book as Open Online Content) at UCL Press. She teaches and researches book and reading history, particularly female owners and readers of Arthurian literature in fifteenth- and sixteenth-century England, and also has research interests in digital academic publishing.

Advisory Board:

Simone Murray, Monash University
Claire Squires, University of Stirling
Andrew Nash, University of London

Leslie Howsam, Ryerson University
David Finkelstein, University of Edinburgh

ABOUT THE SERIES:

This series aims to fill the demand for easily accessible, quality texts available for teaching and research in the diverse and dynamic fields of Publishing and Book Culture. Rigorously researched and peer-reviewed Elements will be published under themes, or 'Gatherings'. These Elements should be the first check point for researchers or students working on that area of publishing and book trade history and practice: we hope that, situated so logically at Cambridge University Press, where academic publishing in the UK began, it will develop to create an unrivalled space where these histories and practices can be investigated and preserved.

Cambridge Elements

Publishing and Book Culture
Children's Literature

Gathering Editor: Eugene Giddens

Eugene Giddens is Skinner-Young Professor of Shakespeare and Renaissance
Literature at Anglia Ruskin University. His work considers the history
of the book from the early modern period to the present.
He is co-author of *Lewis Carroll's* Alice's Adventures in Wonderland
and Through the Looking-Glass*: A Publishing History* (2013).

ELEMENTS IN THE GATHERING

Picture-Book Professors: Academia and Children's Literature
Melissa M. Terras

Christmas Books for Children
Eugene Giddens

Printed in the United States
By Bookmasters